Going The GREYHOUND WAY

The Romance of the Road

Robert Gabrick

Iconografix

Iconografix
PO Box 446
Hudson, Wisconsin 54016 USA

Iconografix books are offered at a discount when sold in quantity for promotional use. Businesses or organizations seeking details should write to the Marketing Department, Iconografix, at the above address.

Library of Congress Control Number: 2009932279

ISBN-13: 978-1-58388-246-7
ISBN-10: 1-58388-246-4

09 10 11 12 13 14 6 5 4 3 2 1

Printed in China

Cover and book design by Dan Perry

TABLE OF CONTENTS

DEDICATION

To Barbara Markham, my friend, colleague, and indispensable research partner

Barbara at last found an interesting transportation research topic. For her a true "romance of the road" travel experience involves handing over the keys of her Dodge Neon and leaving the driving to someone else—just the role Greyhound has long coveted.

Guide for Photograph/Image Acknowledgement

AACA: Antique Automobile Club of America Library and Research Center

GBM: Greyhound Bus Museum Archives

HML: Hagley Museum and Library

MBS: Motor Bus Society Library

ACKNOWLEDGEMENTS

As a young boy in the 1950s, I experienced my own "romance of the road." I enjoyed "going the Greyhound way" from Minneapolis to the farm of my Grandmother Frieda and Uncle Paul. The farm, east of Wyoming, Minnesota, was where my mother Helen was born and grew up. The bus would stop and let me off at the intersection of the highway and the "lake road" to Lake Comfort, a spot which allowed the bus to be off the small-shouldered two-lane highway and only a few yards from the gravel drive up to the farm—virtually "to the door service." I loved to listen to the whine of the diesel engine. I still remember the smell of diesel exhaust and the sight of those distinctive rear windows as the Silversides Greyhound gradually disappeared over the hill and into my memory.

I am deeply grateful for the support and contributions of many individuals and institutions that allowed me to go beyond my personal memories and tell this important story of an American icon.

Located in the birthplace of what would become Greyhound is the quintessential Greyhound Bus Museum, Hibbing, Minnesota, featuring pictorial displays, artifacts, memorabilia, and thirteen historical buses. The support and assistance of Gene Nicolelli, *the* force behind the museum, and Glen Katzenberger, allowed access to historical information, advertising images, and photographs essential to the book.

The Motor Bus Society, devoted to the "collection and publication of information about the history and progress of the bus industry," maintains a library near Trenton, New Jersey. Society member Joe Mahawash devoted considerable time and effort to insure access to the Society's marvelous collection of photographs and Greyhound corporate magazines, newsletters, timetables, and public relations materials.

The Antique Automobile Club of America Library and Research Center, Hershey, Pennsylvania, houses a diverse collection of print materials and photographs that are "devoted to the perpetuation of the pioneer days of automobiling." Kim Gardner, the Librarian during my visits, directed me to the extraordinary collection of bus photographs prominently featured in the book.

The Hagley Museum and Library, Wilmington, Delaware, is "the nation's leading business history library and archives." Jon Williams, Curator of Prints and Photographs, assisted in the examination of the *Nation's Business* Photograph Collection. Marjorie McNinch, Reference Archivist, helped me research the Raymond Loewy Papers housed in the Manuscripts and Archives Department.

Kim Bravo, Librarian of the marvelous Automobile Reference Collection of the Free Library of Philadelphia, Pennsylvania, contributed to the successful search for relevant historical material unavailable elsewhere.

Barbara Thompson, Assistant Manager, Gina Tecos, Librarian and Archivist, and the supportive staff at the Detroit Public Library assisted in utilizing key resources in the incomparable National Automotive History Collection.

Continuing a long and fruitful association, Skip Marketti, Archivist and Curator, and Lori Thornhill, Staff Archivist, provided access to the extensive collection of historical materials at the Nethercutt Automotive Research Library, Sylmar, California.

The Library of Congress, Washington, DC, provided essential archival resources.

Laurie Frank, Roger and Marlys Hammer, and Ray Slagle contributed advertisements and Greyhound ephemera.

While relying on the expertise and assistance of many, I alone am responsible for the factual accuracy and interpretations of this book.

INTRODUCTION

AN ENDURING ICON

GBM

It is hard to imagine an America without the Greyhound Bus. It is an institution woven into the fabric of the nation. It has provided the mobility that Americans have always treasured. When personal transportation was in its infancy and car ownership limited, Greyhound provided "fast," reliable, safe, and economical local and regional transportation for the masses. Increasingly, the company grew in size and scope, developing a nationwide system of transportation offering all that it had at the local and regional level.

The integration of its name and symbol into the cultural landscape reflects its iconic status. People don't say "bus," they say "Greyhound." It becomes a self-evident term, recognized by nearly everyone. Like "Kleenex" it became a generic term. Greyhound stands for all bus travel—regardless of the name of the bus company. Its Greyhound dog symbol is instantly recognizable and part of America's cultural lexicon. Despite profound societal changes Greyhound remains an icon, an essential element of the American imagination.

Its relative decline is part of a larger story of economic, political, and social change. This change offers an opportunity to compare and contrast the past and present. Americans rely less on the bus as a form of transportation as other forms have become more appealing. Bus travel originally offered a romantic voyage with a unique pace and style. People without a car found the bus a very desirable way to travel. The journey was an important part of the experience. Today, it's all about the destination. Getting there in the briefest time possible is the goal of most travelers. The airplane has met this requirement and of course airlines have promoted this desirability. In the past, the journey featured tourist stops for the unique and often very unusual, whether a scenic sight, large ball of string, a curio shop, or motel that consisted of

Indian Teepees. The interstate system bypassed much of this in its quest to provide speed and time saving routes that emphasized efficiency—getting there was important only in terms of the arrival at the final destination. Limited access works both ways—onto and off the freeway. The old routes are now secondary roads, while the interstate stops feature the necessities of high-speed travel—fast food, fast gas "fill ups," and fast service at convenience stores. Everything is a corollary of speed and elapsed time is the crucial measure of travel.

Along the way Greyhound eventually lost the edge. The state of the art architecture of its terminals became the faded remnants of bygone glory. Along with the innovative styling and engineering of a marvelous succession of buses, these hallmark facilities had helped to define the entire Greyhound system and to create an icon.

There were many stops that were not glamorous—a drug store, small café, or hotel in a small town—but they were still part of the larger living network that connected the entire Greyhound system. The destinations in the display above the front windshield often spoke of "far away places with strange sounding names." As a child, I remember the bus that had "Siren" in the destination window. I had only a dim understanding of where Siren was (somewhere in Wisconsin), but I thought it would be interesting to go there. There was an allure and a romance to the destinations and the bus was literally a ticket to them. More importantly, bus travel was a romance in the classic sense of the word—denoting a sense of adventure.

Writing about the international travel experience of the upper classes in the early 20th century, Charles Owen, in *The Grand Days of Travel*, noted "tracks were beaten and paths smoothed but the unexpected often happened and, because the speed of advance was not very fast and every scene differed vividly from the last, there was a sense of adventure and discovery in most journeys." Owen also commented on the exclusivity and isolation of today's "package tour" experience. "A characteristic of the package tour is the protection of the herd of customers from reality. Wherever they go, in bus, airport lounge, aircraft, hotel or restaurant, the environment is stereotyped, synthetic and predictable: temperatures, piped music, table d'hote food, décor and basic amenities are much the same everywhere. The scene and the scenery are viewed passively through glass: through the windows of vehicles, lodgings and places of entertainment." In the "grand days of travel" the focus for the upper classes was on amenity and ambience. Some present day accounts present this experience as a kind of nostalgic paean to a vanished lifestyle. However, it was never economically feasible to offer to everyone the kind of "grand travel" Owen recreates. Intended to be exclusive, if it ceased to be that, it simply would cease to be.

Greyhound's goals were something else—to make travel affordable and accessible to millions—a very democratic notion, and also its recipe for financial success. The amenities would have to be more in line with these goals. The millions who rode the Greyhound bus were the beneficiaries of affordable transportation, comfortable and reliable equipment, and restaurants and hotels that provided wholesome and reasonably priced food and pleasant, if not glamorous, accommodations. While suggesting that as a traveler on Greyhound you were special, Greyhound advertising sought to create a message that offered opportunity for the masses and not exclusivity for the elite traveler.

Initially, land-based travel across America required rides in horse-drawn stagecoaches. Replacing these long and arduous journeys, the railroad offered the traveler new levels of comfort and convenience. Prior to the expansion of paved roads, railroads had the advantage. With the expanded road building programs following World War I, bus travel offered access to locations not served by rail. Bus travel provided flexibility—itineraries could vary. Of course this applies to the areas served by rail, but buses offered many more locations—important natural scenic wonders or your sister's house. Bus travel promised adventure and discovery; a respite or escape from the humdrum and the banality of every day life.

New worlds were possible. Travel for each person represented a unique experience. A trip to Niagara Falls represented an encounter with romance and adventure. Transformation was implicit—your trip would change you—you would never be the same person. Greyhound advertising created an attractive romanticized "reality" with word and image portraits offering enticing places to visit that promised excitement and adventure and the bus as *the* means to get there.

The bus and the road, inextricably linked, depend on the other for the fulfillment of its purpose. The bus, like the automobile, represented modernity—the latest example of technological progress. As promoted by Greyhound, the bus also offered a means to experience the wonders of the continent whether man-made—like great cities, and their built features; historic sights like the Alamo; or the natural world—the Grand Canyon, the Rocky Mountains, Yellowstone or comparable wonders along the east and west coasts. Travel involved encounters with the unique and memorable—something to tell the folks back home when you return. In *The Colossus of Roads: Myth and Symbol along the American Highway*, historian Karal Ann Marling analyzes America's continuing "frontier dream of perpetual movement, escape, and self-transformation." Marling argues that in F. Scott Fitzgerald's *The Great Gatsby*, protagonist Nick Carraway expresses the fundamental basis for "the restlessness of the American people," the impulse Greyhound sought to tap. "As the moon rose higher the inessential houses began to melt away until gradually I became aware of the old island... that flowered once for Dutch sailors' eyes—a fresh green breast of the new world. Its vanished trees... had once pandered to the last and greatest of all human dreams; for a transitory enchanted moment man must have held his breath in the presence of this continent...face to face for the last time in history with something commensurate to his capacity for wonder." Greyhound offered "this continent" to the tourist with the "capacity for wonder." Marling also asserts that, "What compels that wonder is nothing less than a continent, so vast as to be unknowable, beyond all intimacy, of a scale commensurate with nothing save the boundless, intangible limits of the imagination."

Discussing tourist sculpture or "roadside colossi"—a giant "Walk-Thru" fish in Hayward, Wisconsin or Paul Bunyan and Babe, the Blue Ox in Bemidji, Minnesota—Marling declares them to be a "magical passage along a dreamlike road that wends its way out of real time and space, into the realm of imagination." The destinations that Greyhound promoted also represented escape and self-transformation—magical passages "into the realm of imagination" for the traveler.

Greyhound also encouraged travel that included the participation and observance of festive occasions and celebrations that included rituals, games, and pageants that helped to leave the ordinary behind. Greyhound highlighted numerous festivals for potential travelers including the Berkshire Music Festivals, Tanglewood, Massachusetts; the Christmas Regatta, Newport-Balboa Harbor, California; the Latin-America Festival, Tampa, Florida; the National Shuffleboard Tournament, Traverse City, Michigan; the Smelt Run, Boyne City, Michigan; and the Snow Carnival, Manchester, Vermont.

Part of the text for one of Greyhound's 1937 brochures promoting travel to the American Southwest provides the basis for this book's title. The brochure, *Across America*, declared,

"There is a graceful Greyhound coach waiting to carry you over Roads of Romance on a glorious, carefree holiday—or on a fast, time-saving business trip.

Adventure seems to lurk around every corner as you speed along in the sturdy, blue and white Greyhound bus. Here is all the romance of stagecoach days, combined with the thrill of smooth, exhilarating power which comes to the motor coach traveler. All the color and romance, all the scenic and historic interest of this American Wonderland are yours to enjoy when you go the Greyhound way."

Come on, it's time to board the Greyhound for a romantic journey through a changing landscape and a changing America....

ACROSS AMERICA
HISTORIC HIGHWAY ROUTES
THROUGH COLORFUL SOUTHWEST
GREYHOUND Lines

GBM

CHAPTER 1

1914-1929: The Journey Begins

MBS

The initial purpose of the bus company that became Greyhound was necessity—the need to get people to and from places on Minnesota's Iron Range. Those who used the bus service needed a regular schedule at a low cost. The Mesaba Transportation Company provided frequent trips and met a need for inexpensive and convenient service. Residents, and in particular workers, owned few automobiles and relied on the convenient service. For longer trips, it was the railroad that offered comfort, style, and amenities.

The Greyhound Traveler, March 1929, the magazine published for the Greyhound customer, acknowledged this initial purpose. "It was not a great many years ago that the motor bus was regarded as a necessary evil—to be used as a means of travel only when one wanted to go to some out-of-the-way, off-the-beaten-path town or rural community which was not graced with any of the more comfortable passenger carriers. It was in these days that motor buses might justly be referred to as 'Rough Riders.' To stand the wear and tear of such a trip in a bus of doubtful dependability over highways (if so we may favor them) that jolted and bounced a person had to be equipped with about as rugged a constitution as the men in Roosevelt's famous regiment."

Continuing to "toot its own horn," so to speak, the article continued: "At the time few people saw any future for this little 'upstart industry,' and as a matter of fact few people cared to see any future in it. Yet there were people—not many, but some—who, endowed with unusual vision, prophesied that this infant industry moving jerkily and uncertainly over the roads was bound somewhere. They said that one day it would grow up and glide smoothly over every highway in the nation. Today the motor bus is no longer a 'Rough Rider' but a masterpiece in mechanical engineering which rolls smoothly and dependably over the highways—serving thousands of rural communities as it travels between all of the nation's principal cities."

With sufficient wealth and the time to travel in style and elegance, the middle and upper classes generally traveled by rail. Automobiles, as expensive as the typical house, were the provenance of the wealthy. Primitive roads limited opportunities for extensive travel except for the most adventurous. In the early 20th century, technology resulted in changes in the work place with a reduction in the hours worked per day as well as the number of days worked per week. Income for the working class also increased. The availability of more wealth for discretionary spending encouraged this class to spend some of their income for leisure activities including visiting family and friends or taking a vacation. Bus line service expanded to meet this growing demand.

In August 1934, *Fortune* magazine featured the "Story of the great American bus line whose name is Greyhound...The First Bus Company of the Land." The article, "Jitney into Giant," told the story of Greyhound from its very humble northern Minnesota Iron Range origins in 1914, with one Hupmobile, to a bus line of 1,800 buses, serving all but five of the nation's 48 states by 1934. "Jitney" refers to the slang term for 5 cents—a nickel—a common fare for early bus service. Carl Eric Wickman, a Swedish immigrant, lived in Hibbing, "an unvarnished young town in the Iron Range" and worked as a diamond drill operator. The slack time in the mines led him to seek other opportunities. He became the dealer for Hupmobile automobiles and Goodyear tires. Robert Craig Hupp introduced the first Hupmobile prototype at the Detroit Automobile Show in 1909, with the first production model, a two-seat Runabout, offered the following year. 1913 production totaled 12,543. Hupmobile billed itself as "the leader of medium priced cars." For 1914, the Hupp Motor Car Company offered five "'32' H.P." models: a Touring Car, Roadster, Six-Passenger Touring Car, Three-passenger Coupe, and a Delivery Car. Each featured left-side driver controls.

Fortune described Wickman's Six-Passenger Hupmobile Touring Car (base price: $1,200) as "the pioneer woman of bussism." Unable to sell the Hupmobile to others, Wickman "sold it to himself" and did a "small livery business with it." On his first trip he collected $2.25. The business grew. Despite, or because of its success, Wickman sold the Hupmobile to two friends, another diamond drill operator, Andy Anderson and Charles Wenberg, for $1,200. The most popular trip was between Hibbing and Alice. Other taxis that charged what the "traffic would bear," with fares ranging from $1.50 to $3, provided the competition. This business did not fare as well. According to *Fortune*, Wenberg could not drive nor speak "very intelligible English." He sold his interest back to Wickman. Wickman and Anderson then "made the innovation that changed them overnight from taxi drivers to pioneer busmen. They decided to make the run from Hibbing to Alice on regular schedules and charged fifteen cents one way and twenty-five cents for a round trip. Business boomed." The partners bought a second car and established a second route.

In the 1930s the Federal Writer's Project (FWP), part of the Franklin Delano Roosevelt administration's New Deal to combat the Great Depression, began creating a series of guide books promoting travel and tourism and celebrating America and its history and culture. The American Guide Series, concluded in 1941, included a regional guide, *The Minnesota Arrowhead Country*, offering highway tours of the region. Following the format for the guidebooks for each state, the book provided a brief history and current information about the towns, cities, and important tourist attractions for each tour in the Arrowhead region of northeast Minnesota. Hibbing, "the iron ore capital of the world," received four pages of coverage. "Timber cruisers were the first white men known to have visited the region." While these men reported ore outcroppings, the original attraction was lumber. Frank Hibbing "platted a town in 1893" following the discovery of "valuable [iron-ore] deposits." The economic "panic" (today we say "recession" or "depression") of 1893 limited development of the town and mining operations at the Mahoning Mine. By the end of 1894, the improved economy resulted in construction of a railroad to run from the town to the Mahoning open pit. The development of the region's timber and mineral resources attracted large numbers of European immigrants as well as migrants from eastern states.

By the turn of the century, Hibbing's population totaled more than 2,000. As the book explains "the village soon found itself in a dilemma. When platted, a site thought to be south of the iron ore deposits had been selected, but now, beneath its very streets, valuable ore was found. The Oliver Iron Mining Company, a subsidiary of the United States Steel Corporation, already in control of the mineral rights, began to acquire all surface rights." By 1910, as mining operations expanded, the company decided to move the town. "It chose a location a mile south, then known as Alice, and there laid out and built a modern community, with lights, water, sewers, and paved streets. In 1919, the move started. Some of the old buildings were cut into sections, transported piecemeal, and put together again. Churches were towed intact, arriving with spires, pews, and decorations undisturbed." Eventually, expanding mining operations resulted in the razing of all of "Old" Hibbing with the "New" Hibbing occupying the site of Alice. It is likely that some relocation began prior to 1919, in part accounting for the popularity of trips to and from Hibbing and Alice.

Published in 1941, *The Minnesota Arrowhead Country* noted, "More than 73 mines have shipped ore from the district. The Hull-Rust-Mahoning [...], the largest open-pit iron-ore mine in the world, lies almost wholly within the village limits. It is three miles long, one mile wide, 375 feet deep at its deepest point, [and] covers more than 1,100 acres." At the time it had shipped 250,000,000 tons of ore and excavated approximately 231,000,000 cubic yards compared to 232,000,000 cubic yards excavated for the entire Panama Canal project. Mining gave Hibbing many world-class "rewards." An example, still in use, is the current high school—the Hibbing Technical and Vocational High School, a "Monument to Education," completed in 1923. Built with an "Olympic size" swimming pool, indoor track, an auditorium seating 1,805 with a "modern pipe organ," and beautiful murals adorning the walls, it is a reminder of a bygone era of the wealth and largesse of mining corporations.

In 1916, Wickman, Anderson and three new partners created the Mesaba Transportation Company, "the first incarnation of Greyhound." Mesaba represented the name for the portion of the Iron Range that included Hibbing. *Fortune* noted, "In 1915 the two partners had earned $8,000; in 1916, the young company earned $16,000; in 1917 its earnings had risen to about $40,000; by 1918 it was operating a fleet of eighteen busses and was expanding throughout the northern part of Minnesota." The buses consisted of the homemade bodies built by Wickman and Anderson mounted on truck chassis. Longer routes featured closed bodies, while shorter routes had open bodies that utilized side curtains "and even the colder days of the year [buses] could be seen lumbering, their curtains flapping in the bitter wind, across the waste land of the Iron Range." In 1946, for publicity purposes, Greyhound paired an unrestored version of an early bus featuring a "homemade" body mounted on a 1916 White truck chassis and a 1941 Silversides Super-Coach. **[fig. 1]**

Fig. 1. 1916 White and a 1941 Silversides Super-Coach. *GBM*

In 1922, Wickman sold out his share for around $60,000. In 1925 he created the Northland Transportation Company, located in Duluth, buying out small bus lines with a goal to extend service to Minneapolis. One such acquisition brought him Orville S. Caesar. *Fortune* observed that while "Wickman was slow-moving and cautious...Caesar was a ruddy and energetic American go-getter, possessed of a head that buzzed with mechanical ideas. Wickman thought in terms of gradual extensions for his lines; Caesar thought in terms of improved busses, new comforts and safeguards, new popular appeal. Thus they complimented each other; under the spell of mutual stimulation they undertook a furious campaign of expansion and still more expansion. They were in a vital business and they knew it. They expanded not merely because expansion was the vogue, but because they were finding out what the railroads had learned long years before: the key to profits in transportation lies in through routing of passengers. So long as bus travel remained a discontinuous process for the individual passenger, the bus business would remain small potatoes."

The Fageol Motors Company, Oakland, California, first introduced the Fageol Safety Coach in 1922. The company, led by brothers Frank and William Fageol, pioneered the design, the prototype for parlor coach buses eventually offered by most manufacturers. The balloons attached to the bus, the Native Americans posing along one side of the bus, and a team hitched to a wagon on the other side indicates a gathering to celebrate something significant. Information supplied with the photograph offers a date of 1921 with Hibbing as the location. However, the presence of the Fageol and its date of origin suggest the event may be associated with the Northland Transportation Company established in 1922. **[fig. 2]**

Fig. 2. Early Fageol Safety Coach, Hibbing, MN. *GBM*

These 1926 photographs feature a Northland Transportation Company parlor coach bus on the University of Minnesota campus in Minneapolis. Shown outside the Administration Building, the site is now part of the mall that runs from Northrop Memorial Auditorium, built in 1929 to Coffman Union built in 1940. This particular parlor coach body style constituted the design most commonly used by intercity motor coach lines during much of the 1920s. Later versions would adopt and modify features common to railroad passenger cars. **[fig. 3, 4]**

Fig. 3. Northland Transportation Company, 1926. *GBM*

Fig. 4. Northland Transportation Company, 1926. *GBM*

Railroads began to notice the growth of bus companies, often launching campaigns to assert that buses were ruining highways and not paying their fair share of taxes to support highway building and maintenance. Railroad officials generally attributed ticket sales declines to the bus. However, in 1925, Ralph Budd, President of the Great Northern Railroad, supported research in Minnesota to determine the impact of the bus on railroad passenger ticket sales. This research showed that regardless of whether a bus served a community, railroad passenger ticket sales declined by virtually the same rate. Budd concluded the private automobile, not the bus, was the chief cause of ticket sales declines. Railroads and buses could both benefit from collaboration, not competition.

Budd saw the bus as a replacement for unprofitable railroad branch lines and more importantly, buses could also serve as feeders and actually add more passengers to the major railroad lines. In 1926, the Great Northern Railroad bought an 80 percent interest in Northland Transportation for $240,000. Wickman retained 20 percent with the proviso that he continue to operate the company. According to *Fortune* a major effect was that Northland was now "in the hands of large corporations, and with railroad money to back it, could grow into a vehicle not only for transport, but also for large-scale financial operations."

Wickman and Caesar continued to both manage the Northland Transportation Company dominated by the Great Northern and to buy up "literally hundreds of small [bus] lines." This was during the heart of the economic boom of the 1920s. Mergers and acquisitions were commonplace in many industries. The core of Greyhound that was established, however, was not Great Northern-dominated Northland Transportation, but the Motor Transit Corporation set up by Wickman and some ex-partners and others in 1926 to hold the stock of the acquired bus lines. These ex-partners were usually former operators of bus lines originally acquired by Northland who had then split from Northland and sought to establish their own independent bus lines then re-acquired by Motor Transit. In 1930, the Motor Transit Corporation became the Greyhound Corporation, with headquarters in Chicago. Greyhound, however, dates its birth as 1926, with the creation of Motor Transit Corporation. Wickman and Caesar continued to buy up over 100 bus lines in the South and West acquiring the likes of the Blue Goose Lines, the Sunny South Lines, the Royal Rapid Lines, and the Purple Swan Lines.

A third major figure now entered the Greyhound story—"promoter" Glenn W. Traer, Jr., of the investment firm of Lane, Piper, and Jaffray. *Fortune* declared, "Just as Caesar had complemented Wickman, so now Traer supplemented both Wickman and Caesar." Traer's future contributions in the wake of the Great Depression would be crucial to Greyhound's success.

In 1929, Greyhound established additional subsidiaries with other railroads. Southland Greyhound Lines involved the Southern Pacific, the Cotton Belt, as well as the Southland Red Ball Motor Bus Company. The Richmond Greyhound Lines joined with the Richmond, Fredericksburg and Potomac Railroad, while a new Northland Greyhound Lines remained connected to the Great Northern Railroad. The Pennsylvania Railroad also acquired $330,000 in Greyhound stock. Actually, since 1928 the Pennsylvania had been purchasing Greyhound stock. As with the Southern Pacific, an operational arrangement was subsequently established. In 1930, the railroad sold its holdings in Greyhound and set up an operating subsidiary to handle its bus requirements that had been operating as wholly owned subsidiaries. The Pennsylvania Railroad and the Greyhound Corporation each owned half of the stock.

As a result of its acquisition of over 100 bus lines between 1926 and 1932, Greyhound also established Eastern Greyhound Lines of New England, Eastern Greyhound Lines of Delaware, Illinois Greyhound Lines, Central Greyhound Lines, Capital Greyhound Lines, Dixie Greyhound Lines, Teche Greyhound Lines, and Atlantic Greyhound Lines. None of these involved a railroad company. Canadian Greyhound Lines, Ltd., a subsidiary of Eastern Greyhound lines, was also established. The Greyhound Corporation did not have a stock interest in the Canadian company. The details of all the creating and acquiring helps to explain the specific actions that led, as *Fortune* put it, to the creation of the "great American bus line whose name is Greyhound...The First Bus Company of the Land."

While the role of men "endowed with unusual vision," as *Fortune* described Greyhound's leadership, is the crucial element in the story, an even fuller appreciation of the Greyhound saga requires a look at the development of a national network of highways, an element absolutely essential to the visionary creation of a national system of motor bus service. In 1914, when the forerunner of Greyhound began service, only 750 miles of concrete highway existed in the entire United States.

The Lincoln Highway offers an example of the dynamic between idealistic vision and pragmatic reality in early twentieth century road building. In *The Lincoln Highway: Main Street Across America,* Drake Hokanson asserts, "The Lincoln Highway was an expression of the national desire to bind the country from east to west. It captured the nation's imagination [like the] great westward migration on the Oregon and California trails, the pony express, and the transcontinental railroad [...]. Along with the motor car, the Lincoln Highway allowed ordinary citizens the opportunity [...] to make their own journey, to express their own transcontinental aspirations."

The Lincoln Highway was the idea of Carl Fisher, an owner of the Indianapolis Motor Speedway and Prest-O-Lite, articulated in 1912. He initially called it the Coast-to-Coast Rock Highway. As initially envisioned the road's organizers would provide the materials while local groups would provide the labor and equipment and continued maintenance. Fisher had the support of many Indianapolis transportation related manufacturers, but significantly, Detroit's

Henry Ford refused his support. However, Detroit-based industrialist Henry B. Joy, Packard President, offered $150,000. Joy suggested that Congress should consider funding the highway as a monument to Abraham Lincoln. Fisher argued successfully for calling the road the Lincoln Highway. Along with Joy, additional support came from Hudson, led by Roy Chapin, and Willys-Overland. These efforts culminated in the creation of the Lincoln Highway Association on July 1, 1913.

Fisher and Joy clashed on the route of the road, with Joy asserting control and largely determining the road's route. Hoping to generate funding for additional miles of highway Joy advanced the idea of constructing concrete "seedling miles." Constructed in the fall of 1914, the first mile, near De Kalb, Illinois, utilized donated cement and funding. Construction of four more "seedling miles" followed in Illinois and Nebraska in 1915. In February 1915, the Panama-Pacific Exposition, a celebration of the opening of the Panama Canal with the latest in art, technology, and science opened in San Francisco. Joy and others set out on the almost imaginary Lincoln Highway in a new 12-cylinder Packard, taking 11 days to go the 1,000 miles from Chicago to Cheyenne. The total trip to San Francisco required 21 days. Hokanson suggests that for many, the muddy Packard "kindled the flame of adventure," with the car becoming "like some holy relic...different from all those shiny cars nearby; this was a machine that took on mystical qualities because it had done something adventurous, something those gathered at the velvet rope were dreaming about or planning."

However, this rudimentary highway system, little more than a dirt road across the continent, offered travel opportunities to only the affluent few, those with the time to travel and with an income sufficient to purchase a car with or without "mystical qualities" that cost the equivalent of a middle class house. This needs to be remembered when writers lament the changes the interstate highway system has brought. Rhapsodizing and romanticizing about travel in the past too often ignores its harsh reality. Hokanson is in part representative of this genre, offering elegies for a lost America. He contends, "In the past, travelers on the Lincoln Highway traveled deep amid the cultural and natural landscape of the nation.... While there is significant validity in this perspective, those reflecting on past travel need to remember its arduous nature and exclusivity. In the past travelers more often than not "traveled deep amid" *mud* and were less interested in "the cultural and natural landscape of the nation" than in actually arriving at their destination. Greyhound's contribution was to democratize travel, to make it affordable, convenient, and comfortable for the masses. The vast interstate highway system became a means to this end.

In World War I, the United States mobilized with an unprecedented government program of regulation and control. This represented a change in the role of government that became the pattern for the future. When World War I began in 1914, only slightly more than 3,000 miles of hard surfaced road existed in the entire United States—road building and maintenance a local responsibility. Following the pattern of an increased role for the federal government, Congress passed the Federal Highway Act in 1921, providing funds administered by the Department of Agriculture for the development of a system of interstate federal highways. To facilitate highway construction, the federal government also gave over 30,000 surplus trucks purchased for use in the war to various state highway departments. The roads planned and constructed starting in 1921 became, as nostalgically described by Hokanson in *The Lincoln Highway*, the highways "of the diner and café, the road of Burma-Shave signs, narrow bridges...of neon and mom and pop tourist camps, scenic overlooks, and gas stations with all-electric pumps." The development of this road network would be the essential basis for a bus company based on a "national network of lines, cooperating through a mother company"—the model for the Greyhound Corporation.

In the summer of 1928, a bus crossed the country from Los Angeles to New York. This proved to be a crucial event in Greyhound's evolution. Yelloway System operated the bus that made the transcontinental trip. Primarily operating on the West coast, Yelloway, owned by Wesley E. Travis, was in competition with Charles F. Wren's Pickwick Stages that operated as far east as Kansas City. The vision of Greyhound's leadership was to reduce competition and establish a "national network of lines, cooperating through a mother company which would hold, if not the actual majority, then at least an operating control." Greyhound's purchase of Yelloway in 1929 for $6,400,000 provided evidence of this grander vision. Traer got $2,000,000 of the total from the sale of stock to

Fig. 5. Yelloway 1925 White Model 50A. *HML*

86

THE SATURDAY EVENING POST

November 23, 1929

"ROUND HOUSES" along the nation's highways that assure better transportation service

Over 8 million passengers ride in busses every day. This public favor has forced new developments in the operation of economical, safe and desirable highway travel.

To maintain schedules there must be the strategic outposts, fully stocked with parts, completely equipped and adequately manned to serve the minor and major needs of these newer limiteds of the highways.

White builds the most efficient and the most dependable bus that engineering experience is capable of—four and six cylinder models from 12 to 41 passengers for every type of service. White busses offer the greatest luxury in highway travel. Their safety, comfort and on-schedule performance make them the outstanding choice of the traveling public. This preference is proved again and again in mixed fleets—attracting more passenger fares—earning more for the operator.

But equally important to the bus operator is the vast network of White service facilities represented by direct factory branches or dealers that dot the major bus routes throughout the United States.

These service points were built up years ago to make local service available when needed for the widespread use of White Trucks. Today they have become the dependable "round houses" of motor bus transportation —equipped with modern facilities, with a complete stock of parts and manned with experienced personnel. To even approximate such a service an operator would have to make a tremendous capital investment in parts and carry the profit-eating burden of unproductive overhead.

The strategic location of White direct factory branches insures to the large fleet owner and the single owner the same care and attention without loss of time.

A careful analysis of White Bus fleet operations will convince the most critical buyer of White's outstanding leadership—a leadership that could come only from a concern whose resources, ability and intention have always been focused on the broadest phases of motor transportation.

THE WHITE COMPANY, CLEVELAND

WHITE

A COMPLETE LINE OF FOUR AND SIX CYLINDER

TRUCKS
BUSSES

Fig. 6. *GBM*

Goldman Sachs Trading Company. As a result, control of Greyhound moved from the operating and promoting group of Wickman, Caesar, and Traer in Chicago to a financial group in New York. Traer also sold $480,000 worth of stock to the Southern Pacific Company.

In this photograph, **[fig. 5]** a Yelloway 1925 White Model 50A parlor coach pauses for a "photo op." For intercity bus service the basic parlor coach design continued as the industry standard until the 1935 introduction of Greyhound's Super-Coach, the revolutionary Yellow Coach Model 719. Powered by a White manufactured four-cylinder engine, the Model 50A featured a standard 198-inch wheelbase with a 230-inch wheelbase optional. Operated by a foot pedal, the "service brakes" featured drums mounted on the drive shaft. The emergency brakes, operated by a hand lever, featured expanding drums located on the rear wheels. The White Company, with manufacturing facilities located in Cleveland, Ohio, stressed its leadership role as a "pioneer builder," with its "busses in operation as early as 1904." White sales literature declared the Model 50A "is maintaining this leadership. It is attractive, low, powerful, quiet, safe, easy-riding, and dependable." This advertisement features a larger White Model 54A parlor coach capable of seating 38 to 41 passengers. White also included this illustration in a sales brochure referring to the bus as the "Pullman of the Highway." **[fig. 6]**

Prior to Greyhound's acquisition, Yelloway's fleet also included buses manufactured by American Car and Foundry Motors Company (A.C.F.), headquartered in New York City. A.C.F. produced a line of buses that included "Street Car, Double Deck, and Parlor Coach" bodies. A.C.F. sales brochures promoted the "Low, racy, and rounded contours" of this 230-inch wheelbase 1927 Parlor Coach model, noting they gave it the "appearance of speed and strength." **[fig. 7]** According to A.C.F. "The success of the Parlor Car type of coach has been largely due to the extremely attractive appearance, inviting patronage by appealing to a larger group of prospec-

Fig. 7. Yelloway 1927 A.C.F. Parlor Coach. *AACA*

tive passengers." A.C.F. indicated the "Parlor Coach has been developed as the result of careful analysis of the factors of luxury and comfort which contribute to this passenger-attracting quality. These qualities include dignity and fineness of appearance, beauty of line and finish, visible safety and the appearance throughout of having been built expressly for luxurious transportation."

In order to encourage sales of its buses, A.C.F. promoted the notion that "touches of luxury in addition to substantial built-in comforts promote the sale of rides." The more-discerning traveler would select bus lines featuring A.C.F. buses in particular, since they featured nickel hardware, mahogany trim, curved glass rear corner windows, velour linings on ceilings and mohair on the walls, "hand-buffed leather overstuffed upholstery," and ten frosted dome lights. The durable body consisted of "thoroughly seasoned hard wood [framework] with all joints screwed or bolted," aluminum paneling, and sheet steel at the rear corners. However, as with all Parlor Coach bodied buses, baggage storage, located on the roof, was less than ideal. According to A.C.F., a "heavy canvas tarpaulin over the rack" offered protection. Drivers used "folding steps" to access the "baggage rack." The A.C.F. buses featured Westinghouse "metal-to-metal" air brakes on the rear wheels with Bendix mechanical fabric-lined brakes on the front wheels. Hall-Scott Motor Car Company, Berkeley, California, a division of A.C.F., supplied the six-cylinder engines.

In addition to its regular service, some early intercity bus companies offered more affluent travelers additional services and amenities similar to those featured on class-based railroads and steamships. While Greyhound had acquired Yelloway in 1929, officials worried about the competition from Pickwick Stages, Los Angeles, California, noted for the development of unique buses, services, and amenities. Too expensive for outright purchase, Greyhound hoped for a merger with Pickwick. The Southern Pacific Railroad had also entered the bus business, looking to combine its subsidiary with an established independent bus line. In 1929, the Southern Pacific provided funds to form Pacific Greyhound, a company that operated Yelloway, Pickwick, and the Southern Pacific bus line subsidiary. The Greyhound Corp., Pickwick Corp., and the Southern Pacific each held one-third of the stock. As a result, Greyhound operated most of the lines in a territory that covered the western coast to the Rocky Mountains. Western Greyhound Lines also operated bus lines for this group.

Fig. 8. 1927 Pickwick Observation-Buffet motor coach. *MBS*

Pickwick introduced one of its unique buses in February 1927. Borrowing its title from author Charles Dickens, Pickwick Stages published *Pickwick Papers*, "A Monthly Magazine Devoted to Motor Stage Travel." The June 1927 issue featured "The Observation-Buffet motor coach, first of its kind in the world to operate in daily passenger service." According to the advertisement, the coach demonstrated Pickwick's leadership in modern highway transportation. With a kitchen, dining service, radio located in the observation compartment, lavatory and "a dozen other refinements, it is luxurious beyond comparison—yet entirely practical, as proven by years of useful service, with popularity increasing day by day." The Observation-Buffet parlor cars operated twice daily between San Diego, Los Angeles, Santa Barbara, and San Francisco. **[fig. 8]** Information supplied with the photograph declared, "This leviathan of the highways resembles a giant ocean liner." The "glass-enclosed pilot house for the driver...gives him clear vision over the tops of cars ahead of his."

Autobody magazine, July 1927, also covered the unique 258-inch wheelbase parlor coach "designed and built in Pickwick's shops under the supervision of Dwight E. Austin, designer and superintendent." The interior's walnut finish was actually sheet aluminum, "grained to a perfect reproduction of natural walnut." Reflecting observation cars in use on railroads, the 14,500-pound bus featured an actual glass-enclosed rear observation compartment with a "highly polished aluminum grid." What looked like canvas awnings were actually made of metal and painted with blue and gray stripes. This design ele-

Fig. 9. 1928 Pickwick Nite Coach. *HML*

ment continued to be a feature of many parlor coach designs until streamlining in the 1930s made it obsolete. "Perhaps the most novel feature…is the elevated, enclosed cab for the driver. The driving compartment is placed directly in the center of the car and extends about one third of the way over the engine hood." The windshield featured curved glass. The bus provided seating for 28 passengers, with "12 passengers in the lower passenger compartment at the front, a like number in the elevated observation section, while four passengers can use the glass enclosed rear observation compartment."

In September 1928, *Autobody* featured "the new Nite Coach, Pickwick's Dwight E. Austin designed all-metal 26-passenger sleeping coach." According to the magazine, "The coach was not designed as body and chassis but constructed as a single unit. What might be termed the chassis are the 7-in. steel channels at each side," with the entire body structure mounted on these channels. Additional cross members and assemblies provided structural strength and rigidity. Due to extensive use of aluminum and light alloys the 14,000-pound 34-foot 6-inch long by 8-foot wide by 10-foot 3-inch high coach weighed less than other more conventional buses. **[fig. 9]**

The motor coach industry often made implicit and explicit comparisons to Pullman railroad cars and their accompanying amenities and services. Like White bus sales brochures, *Autobody* called the Nite Coach "The Pullman of the highway." Powered by a Hall-Scott engine, it featured 13 compartments accommodating 26 passengers. Service, Pickwick publicity explained, featured a steward and chef, "upper and lower berths for night travel, a wash basin and thermos jug in each compartment," a lavatory located at the rear, and a center aisle to serve all compartments." *Autobody* noted, "Portable tables, similar to those in Pullmans are installed for dining or card playing." According to details in *Pickwick Papers* coverage, Pickwick subsequently created the Pickwick NiteCoach Corporation, Ltd. "to own and lease NiteCoaches to motor stage lines throughout the country on a basis similar to that employed by the Pullman Company." Pickwick referred to these coaches using a single word, unlike the use of two words in most contemporary publications.

Analogous to ship launching ceremonies, Pickwick conducted christening ceremonies for the Nite Coaches. A September 1929 *Pickwick Papers* article described the various events. "First it went to Long Beach and created the greatest furor of any exhibit in the Pacific Southwest Trade and Travel Exposition. Clara Bow, motion picture favorite, played godmother to the car, breaking a bottle of ginger ale over its hood and christening it 'Alsacia.' And the throng that had gathered to watch the 'It Girl' act stayed to examine the coach." When the bus arrived in San Francisco at the Metro Goldwyn Meyer (MGM) Stu-

Fig. 10. Miss Highway Travel christens a Nite Coach. *GBM*

dios, "World's Champion Mayor Jimmie Rolph and Raquel Torres, petite Mexican movie star," all took part in a christening ceremony. Pickwick declared, "The Nite Coach is just about the last word in motor travel."

[fig. 10] At another ceremony, Miss "Highway Travel," six year old Betty Blanche Benningfield christens a Nite Coach, the first bus to leave the new five million dollar Kansas City, Missouri, Union Terminal and Pickwick Hotel. Charles Wren, Pickwick-Greyhound President hosted the ceremony broadcast over the radio station KMBC.

Mary Day Winn took a 10,000-mile motor coach trip that included travel in a Nite Coach. Her account, *The Macadam Trail*, while published in 1931, offers insight about traveling in the Night Coach specifically, and intercity motor coach travel in general. As she explained, a "hen does not cross the road from a desire to get to the other side, [...] it is a quest in search of adventure. My reasons for taking a ten-thousand mile journey by motor bus were analogous to those of the hen. I went Marco-Poloing, exploring romantic by-ways on the cars which now race everywhere, like a busy fleet of inland ships." Winn's reference to travel as "a quest in search of adventure" and to "exploring romantic by-ways" reflects the identification of travel as part of the romance of the road. Her descriptions of the "night coach" and its overnight accommodations and amenities reflect Charles Owens' descriptions of travel in *The Grand Days of Travel*. Since most Americans could not afford to replicate her 10,000-mile journey, she offered mostly dreams for the armchair traveler. Greyhound advertisements, however, offered dreams to those who wanted to get out of an armchair and travel. Democratizing travel meant the greater likelihood that dreams, even if less expansive than Winn's travels, could become a reality for more than a select few.

Referring to motor coaches as "inland ships," Winn evoked comparisons with ocean liners and sea voyages using "captain" to refer to the driver. "The terminals from which the inland ships start have the fascination of harbor fronts; a suggestion of far places and perilous journeying hangs around them. The bus wayfarer feels himself more than just a piece of living freight about to be hauled from one point to another; he is a partner in an escapade. The cars roll in labeled with the names of the ports they touch—Boston, Savannah, Albuquerque, San Francisco; in the East they are 'motor busses', the Middle West, a little grandiose, calls them 'motor coaches'; the Far West, still clinging at the glamour of frontier days, dubs them 'stages.'" One of the pencil illustrations by E.H. Suydam that accompanies the text of *The Macadam Trail* is a Pickwick Nite Coach.

Winn continued, declaring "The 'nite coach' running from St. Louis to Kansas City loomed beside the curb like an ocean liner which had crawled up on land; not a stranded liner, out of its element and helpless, but shining and competent. It contained, I had been told, sleeping accommodations for twenty-six people, with two dressing-rooms and a kitchen. The four rows of windows on each side, the two lower rows round like port-holes, marked four levels of berths. In a high glass-enclosed space over the engine sat the captain, jaunty in a gray uniform, with leather leggings and a useless but highly becoming Sam Brown belt. We took in these details while we waited on the sidewalk amid a wharf-like bustle of departure—friends saying good-by, a conductor scanning yard-long tickets, and a white-coated steward staggering under piles of luggage."

"Once inside the coach, I was able to study the monster's internal arrangements, and came to the conclusion that the whole vast bulk must have been designed by a watchmaker, so minutely had all its details been worked out." In addition, "Ranged along a central aisle were thirteen staterooms on two levels, each room containing two berths about the size of those in a Pullman. As though the inventor had not accomplished enough in planning sleeping-places for so many people, he had added boastful touches to his masterpiece: a shelf in each room to hold toilet

Fig. 11. 1930 Pickwick Duplex. *GBM*

articles; reading-lights; ash-receivers; thermos bottles of cracked ice; even—final miracle—basins with hot and cold running water. Noting these wonders, I glanced around instinctively for the Gideon Bibles and the radios, and felt a vague disappointment that they had been overlooked."

Pickwick later modified the initial Nite Coach, adding to the upper level above the area located aft of the rear wheels. The success of these buses led Pickwick to introduce a new day coach. *Autobody*, October 1930 explained "The practicability of the Nite Coach and its success financially and from an operating standpoint have been conclusively proved in more than a year's continuous service between Los Angeles and San Francisco, and more recently between Kansas City and St. Louis." The Duplex, "designed for day travel only, [provided] a carrying capacity of 53, nearly double that of the ordinary-type motor-coach." *Autobody* featured the photograph shown. **[fig. 11]** The caption declared, "A score of these 'leviathans of the highway' are now operating between the principal cities of this country." Like the Nite Coach, the Duplex featured the same double-deck, staggered compartment plan, a lavatory, portable tables for lunching or card playing, and an interior luggage compartment. Pickwick publicity also emphasized the "removable power plant is

Fig. 12. Pickwick Duplex Observation Coach. *MBS*

Fig. 13. Rear vestibule, C.H. Will Motors Corporation bus. *AACA*

replaceable in its entirety in 15 minutes."

The Pickwick Motor Coach Works, Inglewood, California, promoted the "Pickwick Duplex Observation Coach" to other intercity bus companies declaring, "Whether you want to increase your traffic or increase the profit from the traffic you already have, the most effective single thing you can do is to put the new Pickwick Duplex on your schedule. Duplex increases your profit. First, because it carries more passengers. The additional fares are clear profit. Duplex costs no more to operate than an ordinary coach. It is easier to service, more economical to maintain. Built by motor coach operators, its features are the result of years of operating experience. It depreciates more slowly. Taking all these factors into consideration, it represents a potential increase in profit of 300% over ordinary equipment." The point: "The Duplex will increase your business. Its added comfort, its convenience, its greater safety will bring new patrons. It is the greatest advertisement you can purchase." **[fig. 12]**

The development of these unique buses was part of a larger effort to define the very nature of the intercity motor coach industry. Success depended upon offering travelers the "right" mix of services and amenities. Who would travel on a bus raised questions about class and the ability of the traveler to pay for a particular level of service. While railroads and ships offered a class-based service, a difficulty for bus lines was the relatively limited space available to offer different levels of service. Railroads offered travelers Pullman, "The world's greatest housekeeper." Accommodations included sleeping cars in a variety of configurations: compartments, roomettes, bedrooms, and drawing rooms. In addition, trains featured dining cars, open observation, and later fully enclosed observation lounge cars. Pullman also had conductors, porters, stewards, maids, cooks, and a variety of attendants to serve the needs of passengers. These cars became part of the train's consist. Bus lines offering similar service had to operate separate buses, an expense that proved too difficult to recover.

The very use of the terms "coach" and "parlor coach" for buses that often featured rear observation vestibules—even if only used to store spare tires—and the creation of the compartment-based Observation-Buffet Parlor Car and the Nite Coach with their concomitant amenities and services represented efforts to apply the railroad model to the intercity motor coach industry. **[fig. 13]** This C.H. Will Motors Corporation bus illustrates the incorporation of the features of the railroad car vestibule.

Fig. 14. 1930 Yellow Coach Model 376. *AACA*

Fig. 15. 1930 Yellow Coach Model 376. *AACA*

While the metal grille work features a large circular sign, awnings, and lights similar to those on railroad observation cars, it only provides space for spare tire storage. No access from the bus interior exists. In fact the last row of seats runs the full width of the bus and faces forward. The driver used the ladder to store and retrieve luggage on the roof. **[fig. 14, 15]** The two views of a 33-passenger 1930 Yellow Coach Model 376 illustrate typical parlor coach-bodied buses.

The references Winn makes in *The Macadam Trail* comparing buses to "inland ships" and "ocean liners" offers an example of other efforts to answer the question: "What is a bus?" Such attempts to define the bus and the nature of the intercity motor coach industry in general, while poetic and adding to the romance of the road, did not prove successful. The limited number of customers willing to travel in this manner and pay fares that reflected the additional costs of such amenities and service led to the termination of this kind of service in the later 1930s. Ultimately, the intercity motor bus industry abandoned the class-based model and the compartment-based motor coach. Greyhound's goal of democratizing bus service offering travel opportunities for the masses and not exclusivity for the few became the norm. This is not to suggest that amenities and service were unimportant considerations. The intercity motor coach industry and Greyhound in particular offered comfort and "luxury" for the passenger who stayed in a seat for the entire journey—across the state or across the nation. The stops along the roadside offered the amenities and service a train or ship could bring along with it. The lack of control over their quality eventually led Greyhound to develop the "Post Houses" to provide "low cost restaurant and high standard comfort facilities."

Based on the vision of Greyhound's leadership to establish a "national network of lines," acquisition, development, and definition characterized Greyhound during the 1920s, creating the essential elements of the modern Greyhound Corporation. In *America in the Twenties*, Geoffrey Perrett declared the "Twenties were the first decade of the twentieth century." Characteristics of the decade include what historians label as "modern:" a shorter work week, increased production of consumer goods, higher income levels, more leisure time, a growing middle class, advertising that successfully sought to influence and encourage consumption, mass circulation magazines that utilized advertising revenue to support their viability, credit that allowed immediate instead of deferred gratification, and increased urbanization. Historians also assert the 1920s featured a more national, rather than regional or local, setting of standards, more secular manners and morals, a celebrity culture, a cult of youth, and the emergence of new roles and identities for women. Greyhound grew in part as a result of these significant changes. Greyhound also successfully exploited these changes to help it expand and to increasingly promote the democratization of travel. Despite, and even more importantly, because of the Great Depression, this process continued during the 1930s.

Yellow Coach parlor coach body interiors. *AACA*

CHAPTER 2

1930-1939: Riding Out The "Economic Hurricane"

Author's Collection

Fortune had up to now smiled on Greyhound. Creative and ingenious financing, however, relied on the belief that the economic prosperity of the 1920s was the norm. It was not. In its August 1934 issue, *Fortune* magazine put it this way: "And thus when the economic hurricane struck at the end of the decade the parent company, the Greyhound Corp., began to make heavy weather of it." Specifically, by October 1, 1930, Greyhound Lines earnings were insufficient to pay preferred stock dividends. Such a situation made it difficult for Greyhound to acquire funds for new equipment and other capital improvements. The decline continued. In 1932, the nadir of the Great Depression, Greyhound's operating revenues were 27 percent lower than in 1930.

In part, Greyhound survived the financial "heavy weather" with the help of the General Motors Corporation, a major equipment supplier to Greyhound. General Motors agreed to take over $1,000,000 in Greyhound bank debt. Because of its significant equipment purchases, the survival of Greyhound was also essential to General Motors' survival as a bus manufacturer. *Fortune* explained this relationship noting, "Greyhound busses are almost all built by General Motors Truck Co. In the early days, however, few large truck builders were interested in working out a pioneer, long distance bus, and Greyhound in 1927 had bought out a small Minnesota factory and set up its own bus-building subsidiary, the Will Motor Co. Soon, however, General Motors became interested, bought a 35 percent interest in Will, and had the building of Greyhound busses transferred to its own shops." Differing slightly from this, *Bus Transportation*, January 1930, reported on an announcement made December 7, 1929, a "30 percent interest in the C.H. Will Motors Company [...] has been purchased by the Yellow Truck and Coach Manufacturing Company, a subsidiary of the General Motors Corporation, Pontiac, Mich."

A 29-passenger 1928 Will Model NTB, with a body built by Eckland Brothers, Minneapolis, parked outside an entrance to the Minneapolis Municipal Auditorium **[fig. 16]** and a Yellow Coach Z-250 Model 376 **[fig. 17]** provide examples of the parlor coach buses Greyhound added to its fleet from these two manufacturers. The imprint on the Will photograph indicates the name of the business, headquartered in Minneapolis, is the C.H. Will Motors Corporation—the correct title, despite the two variations in the previous paragraph.

Fig. 16. 1928 Will Model NTB. *AACA*

Fig. 18. Mack Parlor Coach. *AACA*

Fig. 17. Yellow Coach Z-250 Model 376. *AACA*

Fig. 19. Mack Parlor Coach. *AACA*

Greyhound also purchased buses from Mack Trucks, Inc. The 1930 *Back of the Mack*, sales brochure declared, "Builders of the first gasoline motor bus in America, the Mack company has always maintained leadership in the bus field. The present line of Mack buses constitutes the most highly standardized and most completely manufactured offering of heavy-duty buses in the world." Greyhound selected the six-cylinder 126-horsepower 265-inch wheelbase Model BK, heralded by Mack as "the most powerful bus in America."

[fig. 18, 19] Mack buses featured hypoid bevel drive and while not selected by Greyhound, Mack offered optional gas-electric power. As these photographs illustrate, the Mack buses in Greyhound's fleet featured parlor coach bodies reflecting railroad car features. Mack noted the "Bodies are thoroughly standardized along the most modern lines in appearance, accommodations, and structure" and "built upon an all-steel base with wood framing of selected kiln-dried white ash and aluminum paneling outside and within."

Greyhound's operating profit for 1933 totaled $3,111,000, compared to $850,000 in 1932. However, 1933 profits were in part the result of "drastic operating economies," something that could not continue. The 1933 figure also included a $500,000 profit from World's Fair Greyhound, a subsidiary that provided bus service for the 1933 Century of Progress in Chicago. This subsidiary continued to operate in 1934, but its 1933 success led Century of Progress officials to increase their concession fees, diminishing its profitability. "In 1933 busses collected total gross passenger revenue of $283,000,000." Of this total, intercity bus traffic generated close to $177,000,000 with the Greyhound system collecting $27,000,000. By way of comparison, total gross passenger revenue for Class I steam railroads for the same period totaled $331,000,000.

Fig. 20. *GBM*

them learned some years ago to exchange handclasps with the railroads."

The difficult times led others to advocate placing the bus industry under Interstate Commerce Commission (ICC) authority. Greyhound's "biggest asset" consisted of franchises. States had their own regulatory laws and commissions with the power to grant franchises. The franchises, based on a seniority system, could pass from one bus company to another as a result of the sale of a company. The franchises, *Fortune* noted, "must be bought up; and thus it tends to be property far surpassing in value the physical equipment that a line may possess. In its early days Greyhound frequently won franchises merely on application; in the boom days one of them might have cost as much as $100,000." A state bestowed a franchise, but a company could be "forbidden by one state to take on or put off passengers between certain points (because a local, intrastate line held a franchise), but still be quite free to use the highways of the state between terminals that lie outside it." Greyhound's willingness to submit to ICC control was part of its effort to eliminate these regulatory difficulties and the "'irresponsible' little fellow."

In the Great Depression years bus lines competed with each other for a share of ever-declining passenger totals. A problematic solution was to reduce rates. Competing bus companies often willingly competed with each other by lowering rates often below the level of profitability. *Fortune* saw the individualistic bus operators in an industry dominated by "very small companies which do a helter-skelter sort of business" as the problem. These companies did not want regulation since they would be unable to compete if they could not offer lower rates. *Fortune* noted that the stabilization of rates was the "main problem for the immediate future." The article suggested that to increase revenues would require a kind of cooperation among bus operators—to "doff their hat to each other now, in the way the more enterprising of

Bus companies also advertised as a means to gain a larger share of "ever-declining passenger totals." Developed initially in the 1920s and utilized more extensively in the 1930s, a unique style of advertising taught people to become consumers, giving them, as one advertising proponent declared, "the imagination and emotion to desire." In particular, this new style of advertising clearly sought to blur the distinction between wants and needs. Joshua Zeitz in *Flapper*, his "look at the women who launched the first truly modern decade," argues that starting in the 1920s advertisements increasingly offered appealing artwork and copy with the aim to entice the consumer to desire the product or service regardless of need. The visual focus of advertisements, Zeitz notes, "moved away from the product itself toward the image of people enjoying the product." The admen were selling "the happiness and exhilaration that came from buying" the product. "The focus wasn't on the product; it was on the dream that the product held out for its consumers." By the 1930s Greyhound's advertising reflected this style.

In particular, Greyhound advertisements produced during the "heavy weather" of the 1930s offer a view of a company coping with the impact of the Great Depression by, for the most part, ignoring it. Greyhound's advertisements offered dreams, and travel promised their fulfillment by providing "happiness and exhilaration." The consumer knew the reality so the advertisements offered "remedies" for reality—dreams. The world according to Greyhound featured well-dressed travelers having a wonderful time on a Greyhound bus. These Greyhound advertisements provide insight into the minds of those seeking to convince would-be consumers to fulfill their dreams of romantic adventures and for "Going the Greyhound Way." They tap into what Greyhound believed potential customers wanted and even fantasized—promising such things as adventure, excitement, fun, education, new social relationships, comfort, convenience, safety, and a romantic encounter with the open road.

In *Advertising the American Dream,* Roland Marchand argues that advertisements "dramatize the American dream." He contends, "People prefer to identify with portrayals of themselves as they aspire to be." Greyhound advertising offered the consumer portrayals of aspiration. Reflecting back on developments that characterized the 1920s and that despite the Great Depression would later continue to accelerate, increased leisure time and greater disposable/discretionary income meant more people could travel for reasons beyond necessity. Greyhound's audience became the growing number of more affluent middle and working class consumers.

Marchand also notes advertising tells stories through parables and social tableaux using a symbolic language of word and visual images. Advertisements based on social tableaux depict a contemporary "slice-of-life." The result is that the people depicted in the advertisements are like actors with defined roles

Fig. 21. *GBM*

reflecting prevailing norms that play out the script based on age, gender, race and ethnicity, and class. Greyhound advertisements featured a variety of age groups as well as males and females while depicting whites as travelers with blacks limited to providing services. **[fig. 20]**

Generally, Greyhound advertisements featured middle class travelers, but the point is that everyone would want to see themselves as nothing less than middle class. Riding the bus was a fulfillment of dreams—it is what you aspired to and Greyhound sought to convince you that you could afford the trip and thus enjoy the good life. The various tableaux offered romantic places at affordable rates enabling you to imagine your dreams coming true.

The cover of this book features a portion of this 1934 advertisement depicting a variety of social tableaux: A visit to your college, perhaps for a class reunion or *the* rite of Fall, Homecoming and the traditional football game; the Century of Progress in Chicago; a business trip for the successful man of commerce; the man at leisure—hunting. The message: you could be "Going the Greyhound Way" to each of these. **[fig. 21]**

Greyhound advertisements sought to redefine who traveled. By encouraging travel for women,

Fig. 22. *GBM*

Fig. 23. *Author's Collection*

Greyhound offered alternatives to the home, usually defined as the woman's sphere. The man's sphere, the world of business and commerce—the life away from home, continued. Advertisements depicted men traveling for business (not personal/leisure) reasons for the most part. Advertisements offered social tableaux depicting the trip on the Greyhound bus as a desirable use of the increased leisure time and greater disposable income available to women, depicting them as smart and practical-minded, modern, and not foolish or extravagant. Greyhound used testimonial advertisements featuring a fictional person representing a particular consumer group, for example, a female traveler. The ads usually depicted women as independent—financially and socially, unmarried, and a member of the middle class. Women, in particular benefited from labor saving home appliances and products that increased leisure time. Increasing income levels provided more discretionary income. Greyhound wanted the choice of leisure and the money available to result in travel on Greyhound. Women depicted in the advertisements would in general be free from family and homemaking responsibilities. **[fig. 22, 23]**

Fig. 24. *GBM*

Fig. 25. *GBM*

Fig. 26. *GBM*

Greyhound offered affordability for most travelers. While not directly aimed at those who could not afford to travel, Greyhound advertisements also appealed to anyone who would *like* to travel. The advertisements encouraged the daydreams of those who could not afford to travel now to work and save to enjoy this experience in the future—hence promoting character traits identified with success: ambition, hard work, and thriftiness. As a result, we see the dreams that advertising writers/creators thought people were dreaming. Specifically, dreams of travel to go somewhere interesting and exciting—romantic, but also affordable and with people you will enjoy meeting and traveling and spending time with on the bus. **[fig. 24, 25]**

Marchand describes "visual clichés," the visual imagery used in advertising, explaining that such imagery is essential to reverie and fantasy, that is, to daydreaming. He cites Jerome Singer, who argues that daydreams "represent rehearsals and 'trial actions, for all practical future activity.'" Marchand asserts, "By the 1920s in the United States, advertising had become a prolific producer of visual images…a contributor to the society's shared daydreams." The day-

Fig. 27. *GBM*

Fig. 28. *GBM*

Fig. 29. *GBM*

dreams Greyhound offered travelers included opportunities to see both natural and scenic locations as well as man-made achievements such as great cities, buildings, or construction projects. This further reinforced the daydream of the autonomous individual. Travel on the Greyhound bus offered the freedom and the romance of the road. **[fig. 26, 27]**

The Greyhound bus also provided a setting for social relationships. Greyhound advertisements usually depicted travelers as adventurous, independent, and intellectually curious; character traits deemed desirable in many daydreams. Advertisements promoted the fantasy that travel on a Greyhound bus promised a kind of social cohesion for the passengers. The group of travelers could almost become a family on a journey together. While the reality usually offered something far less than these daydreams, who would want to admit it. Travelers might be reluctant to come back home only to tell friends and relatives that the trip failed to live up to the daydream they all shared with the traveler. **[fig. 28]**

Viewed from another perspective, these advertisements also invited everyone to participate in Greyhound travel opportunities. Marchand argues that advertisements tell stories, or "great parables," that draw practical moral lessons for everyday life. One such parable is "The Parable of the Democracy of Goods." Marchand explains, "The wonders of modern mass production and distribution enabled every person to enjoy the society's most significant pleasure, convenience, or benefit." This is a democracy defined in terms of equal access to consumer products, and as a result, a society of "uncontestable equality." Greyhound advertising emphasized motor bus transportation of high quality—the bus was the equivalent of an expensive limousine according to some of its advertisements, featuring amenities such as comfortable seating, conditioned air, and a smooth relaxing ride. As incomes increased, the public sought confirmation of their improved standard of living through consuming products and services of the kind formerly available only to the wealthy. **[fig. 29]**

While not referring to motor bus travel in general or Greyhound in particular, Marchand concludes with a reference particularly apt for travel on roads. "Advertising has served as America's 'green light,' [...] the promise of an open road accessible to consumers." As depicted in its advertisements, travel by Greyhound offered the open road literally and figuratively. Travelers rode the bus and experienced the open

Fig. 30. *GBM*

Fig. 31. *MBS*

Fig. 32. *MBS*

road as a consumer as well as a daydreamer based on their "capacity for wonder." Greyhound hoped to tap both. One advertisement urged the reader to "Follow This Highway" paved with "Informational, pictorial folders covering all America." In particular, "It is a highway paved with advanced information…the bright new folders pictured here are waiting only for you to mail the coupon below." Checking "squares" on the mail-in coupon resulted in recipients receiving folders such as *California* and *Pennsylvania*. The folder covers feature a distinctive artistic style and also reflect prevailing stereotypes. [**fig. 30, 31, 32**]

Greyhound published a variety of brochures and folders for the traveler. Due to their expanded format, these promotional materials offered important facts and details—fares, destinations, contact information, and other details about aspects of motor bus travel—all providing guidance and factual information needed by the consumer. Marchand observed, "Advertisements depict and describe the material artifacts available for purchase at a given time. They reveal the state of technology, the current styles in clothing, furniture, and other products, and sometimes the relative prices commanded by various goods." Greyhound advertising provides a view of all of these factors.

Fig. 33. *MBS*

Fig. 34. *MBS*

Fig. 35. *MBS*

Down the Highway By Greyhound

Down the Highway By Greyhound, a brochure published in the early 1930s, offered an extensive and informative look at "modern bus travel," suggesting a significant segment of the population was uninformed about the basics of bus travel in general and Greyhound in particular. The brochure provided answers to this question: "What can a traveler expect when traveling on Greyhound?"

Expect to see natural and man-made wonders. Travelers will see a majestic waterfall and by contrast New York's Empire State and Chrysler buildings and Rockefeller Center. The Greyhound bus connects the two, the means to see both kinds of wonders. **[fig. 33]**

Expect the most modern bus, a competent driver, and passengers you will enjoy. The first page offers "An invitation hard to resist! The trim blue-and-white bus, with its door swung wide—an alert and pleasant driver waiting to help you aboard—the motor purring sweetly in anticipation of miles that will soon surge by. Inside—the kind of passengers you'd like for company on any trip—the most restful chairs in any public vehicle—unlimited view through wide windows on four sides...." The driver's appearance conveys competence, authority, and the ability to handle any situation, establishing trust. The uniform's military-like appearance including Sam Brown belt, boots to just below the knees, jodhpurs, officer's brimmed cap, and bow tie provides visual confirmation. **[fig. 34]**

Fig. 36. *MBS*

Fig. 37. *MBS*

Fig. 38. *MBS*

Fig. 39. *MBS*

Expect the highest degree of safety from personnel and equipment. The brochure also focused on the training for its "Clean-cut gentlemanly drivers." Specifically, "not less than 15 days intensive schooling is given each new Greyhound driver." Drivers received awards for their safe driving with buttons and cash bonuses. "More than 2,000 skilled mechanics and other employees, working in almost 200 big Greyhound garages, hold it a point of honor to keep buses in their territory spotless and mechanically perfect." In addition, passengers can expect to ride in a clean bus. "Buses entering terminal garages for repair and inspection are subject to thorough cleansing and renovation. Window drapes and upholstery are vacuum cleaned—fresh new covers are placed on the chair backs." **[fig. 35]**

Expect transcontinental-wide service of the highest standards. Within the context of the "Astonishing Growth" of motor bus transportation, the text declares, "Head and shoulders above the field are the Greyhound Lines" offering "one standard of safety, one code of honor, one efficient service." The map offers a look at the transcontinental routes traveled by "Smooth-rolling streamlined Greyhound buses." **[fig. 36]**

Expect "Prompt Courteous Information." Greyhound provided "Many complete travel bureaux [...] established for public convenience." The brochure also provided a list of the offices of the Greyhound Lines. **[fig. 37, 38]**

Expect that Greyhound exercised the same care in the selection of facilities wherever they traveled with convenience an important criterion. "Speaking of convenience—it's a genuine relief to step out of a modern Greyhound bus and find yourself right in the heart of the business, shopping and theatre district of a city! That's where you'll find each Greyhound terminal—saving many steps and extra cost. They are always close to good hotels—often in the same building." In addition, "Smaller depots and offices are selected with the same care used in large terminals. In cities and towns where lunch counters or restaurants are not actually installed by Greyhound Lines, depots are established in direct connection with reputable restaurants where the best food is quickly available." **[fig. 39]**

Expect that the romance of the road will be part of the experience of traveling by Greyhound. While the brochure focuses on "Your choice of many romantic highways down through Dixie," the implication is that romantic highways exist throughout America. Greyhound also offered "liberal stop-over privileges." **[fig. 40, 41]** The brochure also includes

Fig. 40. *MBS*

Fig. 41. *MBS*

Fig. 42. *MBS*

FOLLOW COLORFUL PIONEER TRAILS

AN ANCIENT PUEBLO IN NEW MEXICO

THERE'S COMFORT IN THESE CHAIRS!

EVER sink back in the cushions of a late type Greyhound bus chair? If you haven't, a new experience in riding comfort awaits you! The cushions are inches deep, upholstered in rich fabrics. Each chair has a comfortable head rest, covered with fresh white linen.

Chairs are adjustable to any desired position. Just press a button on the chair arm, or touch a foot pedal, and the seat back reclines . . . one position for observation or reading . . . another for relaxation . . . another for restful sleep. This explains why thousands of people prefer Greyhound for all night trips, securing ample rest and sleep in these reclining chairs. Passengers say: "Most comfortable seats in any vehicle."

On cold days, a flood of warm air is poured into each bus from famous Tropic-Aire heaters . . clean air circulated through hot water radiators at front and rear of each car.

Page 12

Fig. 43. *MBS*

Fig. 44. *MBS*

the "Land of 10,000 Lakes" in Minnesota—Greyhound's birthplace, a New Mexico pueblo, and Redwoods in California. **[fig. 42, 43, 44]** The traveler can also expect part of the romance of the road is to travel on "Highways that Made History." These "great highways of America, now smoothly paved and graded, began life as dim trails, beaten by pioneers such as Daniel Boone, and developed by the drift of land-hungry settlers who trekked Westward in covered wagons." While traveling on romantic highways, the traveler should expect comfort on a Greyhound bus. Following the paths of pioneers—thankfully not in a covered wagon—the brochure asks, "Ever sink back in the cushions of a late-type Greyhound bus chair? If you haven't, a new experience in riding comfort awaits you." For those cold days expect "a flood of warm air."

Expect Greyhound to be a "good citizen." Critics, especially railroads, often accused the motor coach industry of not paying its fair share to construct and maintain the highway system. While not a concern of the typical traveler, Greyhound devoted space in the brochure to reassure the traveler they could expect Greyhound used tires that "are kind to the roads" and was "doing its fair share [of] lifting an immense burden from the shoulders of private taxpayers." **[fig. 45]**

• AND ALL THE PACIFIC COAST

Amazing Facts about the Motor Bus and YOUR Highways

IT is a satisfaction to know that the transportation system on which you are riding is doing its fair share and more toward the construction and upkeep of the highways it uses, lifting an immense burden from the shoulders of private taxpayers.

PAYS MORE THAN SHARE OF HIGHWAY UPKEEP

Every State has some method of adequately taxing the bus industry. For example, the gasoline tax in all States averages 4 cents per gallon. Then there are special taxes, licenses and fees that bring the average yearly tax up $575.00 *for each bus*. This is 22½ times as much as the tax paid by the average private car, and 11 times as much as paid by the average truck!

Greyhound Lines pay even a higher tax than this . amounting in many cases to more than $1,000.00 per year for each bus.

The total tax on common carrier buses in one year amounts to 36 million dollars . a huge sum which goes almost entirely to the construction and maintenance of highways which the public uses. Bus lines pay 7.2 percent of their total revenue for taxation . while all other public utilities average only 4½ percent.

Here's an even more astonishing fact, secured by the American Automobile Association:

Motor Buses pay more than 40′ of upkeep costs on highways which they use.

BALLOON TIRES EASY ON HIGHWAYS

Every Greyhound Bus is equipped with 6 huge, low pressure balloon tires. Here is what the United States Bureau of Public Roads says about such equipment: Motor bus balloon tires are from 20′, to 30′, less destructive to roads than high pressure tires on private cars. The motor bus does not leave the road and come back with a hammer blow, as does the ordinary private car.

ECONOMIC NECESSITY . COMMUNITY BUILDER

In the "good old days" people cried out against the first steam trains because, "The sparks will set our field on fire." They told Robert Fulton that his floating tea kettle would surely sink. The livery stable man laughed to scorn the first noisy, one cylinder automobile. Many of us remember when the man who thought it possible to fly was a fanatic! But the steam train, the steamboat, the automobile and the airplane have gone marching on to success.

The motor bus, too, is an economic necessity . a community builder. It offers millions of taxpayers who do not own automobiles their *only* opportunity to use the great highways. The motor bus gives hundreds of towns and communities their only public transportation. It is greatly reducing the cost of travel, while contributing to good roads and highways. Who can doubt that it is one of the most important factors in our National life?

Fig. 45. *MBS*

THE HIGHWAY TRAVELER

Greyhound published the bi-monthly *The Highway Traveler* "for the entertainment of the traveling public and to promote interest in travel through description of scenic attractions and sections of the North American continent." Essentially one large advertisement, the magazine's covers provide examples of what the editors thought would be enticing to the traveler. Despite the admonitions not to do so, readers often do judge a book—or magazine—by the cover. As a result, the cover of *The Highway Traveler* needed to make a positive first impression encouraging the reader to delve into the magazine and more importantly decide to travel by Greyhound bus. A sampling of various 1930s covers reveals recurring themes and subject matter. *Images courtesy Motor Bus Society*

The Great Depression of the 1930s significantly changed the way many thought of and described the highway. No longer just a means to seek romantic adventure and explore America's wonders, the road also became a symbol of displacement and difficulty as migrants escaped the Dust Bowl to seek greener pastures. People sought new opportunities in California, the story told by John Steinbeck in the *Grapes of Wrath*. Oddly, our primary visual images of the Great Depression come from the photographers who worked for the Farm Security Administration (FSA) established by the Franklin D. Roosevelt administration. FSA photographs featured poignant scenes of displaced travelers driving dilapidated automobiles, stopped in makeshift roadside camps, and toiling at work that offered little financial security. Such scenes seem to fit the years prior to the helping hand of various New Deal programs. In fairness, the photographs indicated the problems that still needed attention and provided support for a greater effort on the part of the government. This side of the Great Depression, of course, never found its way into Greyhound's promotional efforts.

While documenting the devastation caused by the Great Depression, some agencies of the New Deal also offered another side of the story. The Federal Writers' Project (FWP) contributed a view more in keeping with Greyhound's vision. In all, the FWP by the end of its existence had created over 400 volumes in the American Guide Series that included guidebooks for each state, as well as regions, cities, and significant highways. Historians such as Christine Bold, in *The WPA Guides: Mapping America,* mine these volumes for such things as "complex cultural processes," "federal intervention into local image-making, and the cultural fallout from the New Deal mapping of public space." Bold asserts that the image of America the guidebooks "fostered is closer to fabrication than to actuality." While the same assertion applies to aspects of Greyhound advertising, ultimately the traveler encounters "actuality." Both the guidebooks and Greyhound advertising optimistically encouraged the ordinary American to celebrate the nation's culture and history and to consider traveling.

The inside flap of the dust jacket of *A Guide to Key West*, for example, explained that it would provide practical details to help travelers encounter romance—as did Greyhound. "This American Guide Series book tells you everything about this island of romantic legend; where to go, what to see, why and how. Thirty-two pages of gravure illustrations and a thorough text prepared from all available sources recount its picturesque history, describe its life and culture, its industry and commerce, and to tell what to look for in the winding lanes and sudden narrow alleys throughout the island." **[fig. 46]**

Designed with the automobile traveler in mind, the American Guide Series was useful for any traveler—including those who rode the bus—interested in America's heritage. In the Forward to *Indiana: A Guide to the Hoosier State*, Ralph N. Tirey, President of the Indiana State Teachers College, explained, "the people of the United States have come to the realization that there has been slowly developing a heritage peculiar to themselves. Steps have been taken to probe into the sources of this heritage, and to seek to discover its component elements. The American Guide Book Series is such an attempt."

The Preface of *California: A Guide to the Golden State* explained that the "editors have tried to make this book a true mirror of the State and its people." Alluding to a theme common to the reader of Greyhound publicity, the preface continued: "Romance

Fig. 46. *Author's Collection*

Fig. 47. Mounds Park, St. Paul, Minnesota. *GBM*

The tour paused on "The Longest Swing Span in the United States" located at La Crosse, Wisconsin. *GBM*

has been kept in its place—Joaquin Murrieta [California's "most notorious bandit" killed in 1853] does not jump out from behind every tree or boulder in California to hold up travelers, and yet he does pop up often enough that the observant reader will have little trouble finding him." If the armchair traveler finds romance, especially reading about a bandit, romance is even more likely for the actual traveler.

Starting in 1935, the Federal Art Project (FAP), part of the New Deal's Works Progress Administration (WPA), produced millions of posters promoting travel. FAP/WPA artists created posters for the United States Travel Bureau and the National Park Service, both part of the Department of the Interior.

In 1930, during the initial phase of the Great Depression and prior to the efforts of the New Deal to promote travel, Greyhound produced a series of publicity photographs featuring Northland Greyhound bus number "700" as it traveled in Minnesota and Wisconsin. While Greyhound would seek to put its best foot forward to promote the romance of going the Greyhound way, the photographs also depict a highway system very much a "work in progress."

Based on the "photo-op" locations it is possible to suggest the most likely itinerary. The bus probably started its publicity tour in St. Paul, Minnesota, traveling south on Highway 10/61, then along the Mississippi River on Highway 61, crossing it to enter La Crosse, Wisconsin. Through La Crosse the bus would follow Highway 53 north to Highway 10 at Osseo, Wisconsin, then west on Highway 10 to Prescott, Wisconsin, continuing on back to St. Paul.

Shown, possibly at the start of the trip, the bus pauses to allow passengers to overlook the Mississippi River in an area of eastern St. Paul known as Mounds Park, due to the presence of Indian burial mounds (including in all probability such a mound at the right in the photograph). The bus will head eastward on Hudson Road, then travel southward on Highway 10/61, taking Highway 61 from Point Douglas, Minnesota, to La Crosse. **[fig. 47]**

In La Crosse, Wisconsin, passengers look over the Mississippi River. *GBM*

The bus has paused at what appears to be a memorial—probably to soldiers of World War I—at an undisclosed location. It is uncertain if the photographer is on the main road or if the unpaved road that leads off into the distance is the highway used by the bus. *GBM*

The bus is heading north at the border of Trempealeau and La Crosse Counties in Wisconsin on Highway 53/35. **[fig. 48]** Highway 53 ran to International Falls, Minnesota, on the border with Canada. Starting as a distinct highway in La Crosse, it continued northward to intersect with Highway 10 at Osseo, Wisconsin. Had the tour continued north instead of turning west onto Highway 10 it would have passed through Eau Claire, Chippewa Falls, Rice Lake, Spooner, and Superior, Wisconsin, continuing through Duluth and Virginia, Minnesota, northeast of Hibbing, on its way to the border at International Falls. The highway is typical of paved, hard surface highways in 1930—two narrow lanes lacking shoulders.

Now replaced in many places by Interstates 90 and 94, in 1930 Highway 10 ran from Detroit to Seattle. It traveled across Wisconsin from Manitowoc on the western shore of Lake Michigan to Prescott on the western border with Minnesota at the confluence of the St. Croix and Mississippi Rivers. In Minnesota, Highway 10 initially joined Highway 61 just across the Mississippi from Prescott, Wisconsin, continuing as a distinct highway through St. Paul as it worked its way west through St. Cloud and Moorhead and into Fargo, North Dakota. The scene shown is in the area near Ellsworth ,Wisconsin to the east of Prescott. As the photograph indicates, this major road still featured unpaved sections. **[fig. 49]**

On occasion, later public relations efforts to tell the story of these years tends more toward wistful nostalgia and factual error than reality. Greyhound publicity, developed in the 1970s for the 1931 Model BK Mack, part of the Collectors' Classics fleet of restored Greyhound buses, provides an example. "1931. It may be the height of the Great Depression—but you're not depressed. Far from it. You're flying past cows and cornfields, taking your very first cross-country trip on Greyhound's new Mack bus." This description, while reflecting advertising hyperbole, could reflect an actual 1931 bus trip. "Are other passengers just as excited? Hard to tell. The ladies all sit up straight, looking proper in their hats and white gloves." While removed inside the bus, ladies usually wore hats and gloves. "The men are engaged in conversation about the New Deal, the C.C.C. and the W.P.A." Wrong! The New Deal with programs that

Fig. 48. Highway 53/35, Western Wisconsin. *GBM*

Fig. 49. Near Ellsworth, Wisconsin. *GBM*

included the Civilian Conservation Corps (CCC) and the Works Progress Administration (WPA) began to take shape following Franklin Delano Roosevelt's election victory in November 1932 and inauguration in March 1933. Herbert Hoover, elected in 1928 and inaugurated in 1929, is President in 1931. Passengers are more likely to be expressing grave concern over the state of the economy, as well as their own good fortune to have sufficient funds to be traveling despite the Great Depression.

The 1930s era offers an opportunity for an exploration of two distinct visions of America. The dystopian vision focuses on the Great Depression and the difficulties for those millions caught up in its effects. Despite their aim to encourage increased efforts to alleviate the problems of the Depression, the subject matter of many of the FSA photographs reinforces the dystopian vision. Some observers, fatalistically, chose not to look beyond that reality. The second vision, more reflective of the FWP guidebooks and the FAP travel posters, was utopian. While acknowledging the difficulties of the Great Depression, these views focused attention on the tremendous increase in creativity and the effort to offer alternatives to hopelessness and despair. The fairs and expositions of the 1930s that Greyhound eagerly sought to persuade travelers to visit promoted a variety of utopian visions.

Another undisclosed location somewhere along the Mississippi River—judging by the hills in the distant background. *GBM*

In May 1933, A Century of Progress opened in Chicago. The *Official Guide Book of the Fair* declared, "the interest of a considerable part of the civilized world is focused upon 424 acres of land that lie along the shore of Lake Michigan, edging Chicago. A little while ago this site was a placid lake. Now, shimmering beside the water, a dream city is risen. It lights the sky with splendor, yet soon will disappear and be merely a memory." In the midst of the Great Depres-

The photograph on the left features a restored bus, while the right photo shows a Model BK in 1930. *GBM*

sion, Greyhound sought to transport travelers to this "dream city." Greyhound actually played two roles at A Century of Progress, getting visitors to the fair and transporting them around the fair during their visit.

The idea for a celebration of Chicago's centennial dates to August 1923 with an initial corporation established in January 1928, and a subsequent name change to "A Century of Progress" in July 1929. While planned prior to the full impact of the Great Depression, the *Official Guide Book* noted the fair celebrated Chicago's progress, declaring "A Century of Progress intends to bring assurance that the steady march of progress has not, however, swerved aside, nor even been seriously retarded, that so-called 'recessions' are temporary, like the cloud that for the moment, obscures the sun. History holds the evidence that this is true." The *Official Guide Book* proudly explained, "A Century of Progress was completed without one cent of taxation being imposed upon an already heavily burdened citizenry. No Federal government, state, county or city subsidy was asked for, or received." **[fig. 50]**

While the fairs offered utopian visions of the future they also prominently displayed the latest examples of progress currently available. The *Official Guide Book* declared, "As two partners might clasp hands, Chicago's growth and the growth of science and industry have been united during this most amazing century. *Chicago, therefore, asked the world to join her in celebrating a century of the growth of science, and the dependence of industry on scientific research.* An epic theme!" "That is the theme of the Fair—*achievement*, and its *promise*." Greyhound sought to create connections between the utopian dreams offered by A Century of Progress and the various fairs and expositions of the 1930s and

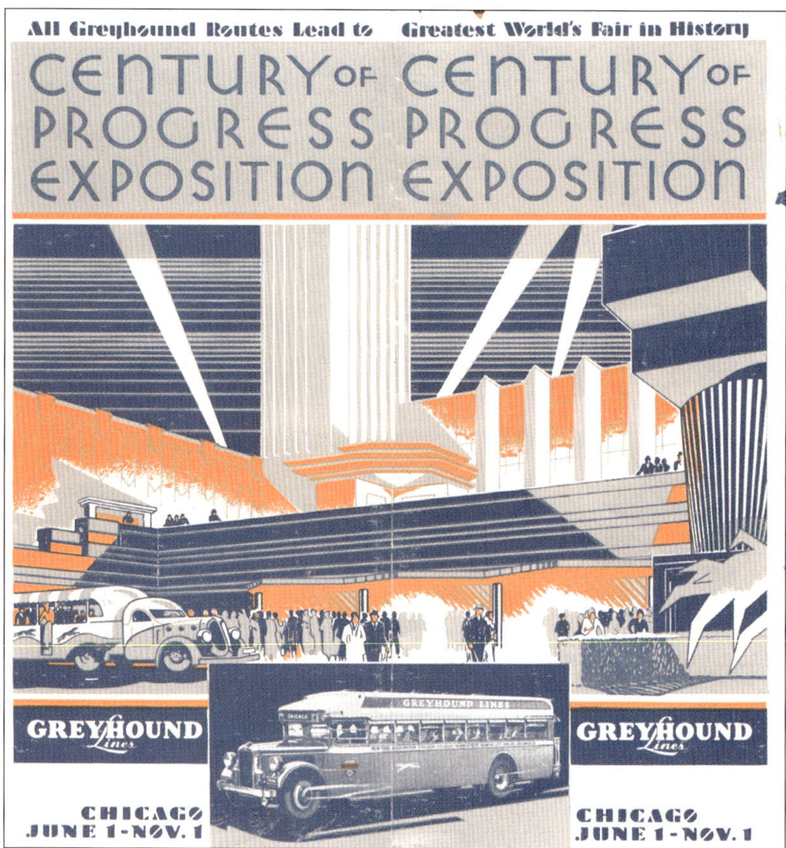

This Greyhound brochure cover features the Century of Progress. *AACA*

Fig. 50.
Author's Collection

The cover of Greyhound's June/July 1933 *The Highway Traveler* promoted the fair, depicting a Greyhound fair bus against a background of exhibition buildings. *MBS*

its own equipment. The vehicles that operated in the fairs reflected the latest ideas in design and engineering, examples of utopian promises actually achieved.

The *Official Guide Book* offered a photograph of "A Greyhound Intra-Fair Bus" loading passengers and reassured visitors, declaring, "When you enter the grounds, transportation is quickly available. Water craft, great, specially built motor buses, wheel chairs, jinrikishas, offer you comfortable means of conveyance. Sixty Greyhound 'auto-liners,' whose full capacity each is 100 persons, were especially designed and built for service in the grounds. These buses operate for your convenience in two ways. If you enter, for example, at the North entrance, and wish to get speedily to the south end of the grounds, you may board a bus that operates in a fenced-in speed lane for through service, with stops only at the Twenty-third street area, and the Maya Temple area near Thirty-first street. The loading area is at your right as you enter the grounds. Other buses, leaving from the east side of the North entrance, operate more slowly, going around on Northerly island, and permitting you to reach any point you desire. The seats of the buses lie lengthwise, and face outward, permitting passengers a full view." *Bus Transportation*, May 1932, reported the sixty buses cost $300,000. The article noted, "The design for the unit follows the general modernistic architectural scheme of the Fair buildings. They will be stream-lined and painted in bright, attractive colors, which will harmonize with the general color scheme of the Fair grounds and buildings." **[fig. 51]**

Fig. 51. Greyhound Intra-Fair Bus. *AACA*

Lisa D. Schrenk, in *Building a Century of Progress: The Architecture of Chicago's 1933-34 World's Fair* asserts, "The sixty open-sided Greyhound Intra-Fair Auto-Liners that moved visitors through the park provided one of the most conspicuous examples of streamlining at the exposition. The two-tone paint schemes on the rounded bus cabs helped produce the illusion of a sleek aerodynamic form." While Schrenk indicates "the aerodynamic aesthetic of streamlining was more prevalent during the fair's second season, with the 1934 appearance of Burlington's *Zephyr* and the Union Pacific's *M10000*, it is still difficult to accept her assertion that the Auto-Liners 'provided one of the most conspicuous examples of streamlining.'" In reality, as the illustrations indicate, Greyhound's "Auto-Liners" were tractor-trailer units developed by General Motors Truck Company, Pontiac, Michigan, in 1932. Streamlining is limited to the paint scheme and the rounded ends of the trailer and the modifications made to the cab of the tractor. The 46-foot 5-inch long units provided seating in the trailer for 50 passengers with standing room for an additional 40-50. According to information released by A Century of Progress, developers selected these units due to the physical constraints of the 2.7-mile long site that in some locations was only a few hundred feet wide, declaring, "All other types of transportation would have cost too much."

The Travel and Transport building designed by John A. Holabird, Edward H. Bennett, and Hubert Burnham provides the backdrop for Greyhound's General Motors Corporation tractor-trailer Auto-Liner. Greyhound featured this photograph in its *All About the Chicago World's Fair* folder, promoting A Century of Progress as the "Greatest Show on Earth!" According to the *Official Guide Book*, "For the first time in architectural history a dome has been constructed on the principle of a suspension bridge. Just as a suspension bridge has no pillars, columns, or arches to support it from below but depends on cables to carry its load, so the dome of the Travel and Transport building is suspended 125 feet above the ground by cables attached to twelve steel towers. The reason for the daring use of this suspension principle was the necessity for a clear, unobstructed space for the exhibits." The 1933 Fair also featured vivid colors for the exhibition buildings. The dark façade of the Travel and Transport building was green. In 1934, the use of color lessened considerably and the building became white. **[fig. 52]**

Greyhound created World's Fair Greyhound, a subsidiary to provide the bus service. *AACA*

Fig. 52. Greyhound/General Motors Auto-Liner. *AACA*

"Of course you'll come to The Fair. You mustn't miss it! You'll forget the commonplace as you delve and revel in the strange and—to you—the outlandish. You'll be whisked about the lovely grounds of A Century of Progress, borne where you will on Great Greyhound Buses—marvels which, in themselves typify to perfection a century of progress in transportation." The Bendix Products Corporation advertisement in Greyhound's *The Highway Traveler* magazine accomplished two things. It informed readers and thus potential travelers that "At the Fair as on the highway...Bendix Safety guards your Greyhound ride!" The Greyhound Auto-Liners shown in the advertisement featured "Bendix-Hydraulic Brakes plus Bendix-B-K Vacuum Power Brakes." In addition, the advertisement featured an illustration of "the temple of Jehol, re-created for A Century of

Fig. 53. Greyhound/General Motors Auto-Liner. *AACA*

Progress, an exact replica of the original edifice. Contributed to the Exposition by Mr. Vincent Bendix." The *Official Guide Book* identifying the structure as the Bendix Lama Temple explained the "Golden Pavilion, the original of which was built in 1767 at Jehol, summer home of the Manchu emperors from 1714 until [1913] was brought to the [Fair]...by Vincent Bendix, exposition trustee. Exact reproductions of the 28,000 pieces of which the Temple is composed were made and numbered at its original site in China." **[fig. 53]**

The Highway Traveler, June/July 1933 featured "A Century of Progress Visitor's Guide." The heavily illustrated sixteen-page article offered a complete overview designed to inform and thus entice travelers. The article noted, "There are some sixty buildings given over to free exhibits, with a total corridor length and walking distance of 82 miles. There are some 12,000 exhibits, so that if two minutes were devoted to the scrutiny of each one it would require six weeks to see them all, working 10 hours a day." At the conclusion of the Visitor's Guide, potential visitors were informed, "No automobiles will be permitted on the Fair Grounds, but the trip from one end to the other can be made on Greyhound observation buses," the Auto-Liners. **[fig. 54]**

The interior of the Greyhound Auto-Liner trailer looking back along the two outward facing bench seats designed for 22 passengers on each side. A bench at the rear provided seating for an additional six passengers. The ride around the entire 424-acre Fair site took approximately 20 minutes. **[fig, 55]**

Fig. 54. Greyhound/General Motors Auto-Liner. *AACA*

Greyhound offered "All-Expense World's Fair Tours" for A Century of Progress visitors. In *The Highway Traveler*, June/July 1934 issue, Greyhound's own advertisement declared that their tours "Saved dollars, time and worry for thousands of visitors last year... This year offers bigger values than ever... Finer entertainment features... Assured hotel accommodations... All expenses in Chicago except meals and transportation." Other tours included stops along the way at Niagara Falls, the Grand Canyon, Yosemite Park, and many other attractive tourist spots on the different Greyhound routes. Advertised

Fig. 55. Auto-Liner trailer interior. *AACA*

in national magazines and local newspapers, they became the basis for Greyhound's Highway Tours promoted prior to World War II. To sell these tours, Greyhound set up travel agencies in many key cities and towns, not only in the U.S. but also in Europe and South America. These tours became a key part of Greyhound's long haul traffic, which for the industry as a whole accounted for only 3.4 percent of tickets sold but 25 percent of revenue.

This advertisement addressed the Great Depression's impact on travel budgets. **[fig. 56]** The advertisement asserts that despite reduced budgets it did not mean you could not travel to "brand new places, stop at the best resorts, thrill to fascinating new scenes…and do it at a fraction of last year's outing." While the assumption that the reader traveled "last year" is problematic, the advertisement suggests, "Chicago's marvelous Century of Progress Exposition heads the list with new low excursion fares and attractive All-Expense tours as extra inducements." Obviously, much of Greyhound advertising promoted dreams and wish fulfillment. This advertisement also offered something for children or the child in every adult. "Here is the cleverest souvenir of the Century of Progress Exposition you ever laid eyes on. An exact replica of the famous stream-line trailer-type buses used only on the World's Fair grounds at Chicago. Sturdy cast metal, modernistic colors, rubber tires, 15 inches long…a wonderful toy and a lifetime keepsake."

Greyhound often used the *Saturday Evening Post* for advertisements to entice potential travelers. This advertisement promotes "The greatest World's Fair of history" as an opportunity that "comes only once in a lifetime." The advertisement highlights the "Nearly

Fig. 56. *GBM*

four thousand modern Greyhound motor buses…pointed toward the Century of Progress Exposition at Chicago" that "remove the last faint doubt about your ability to attend." The traveler can attend because "going the Greyhound way" is affordable. "Greyhound fares are immensely lower than other first class transportation […] less than a third the cost of operating a small private car." In addition the traveler would enjoy "the first-hand beauty of America" in "the comfort of reclining cushioned chairs" en route to the Fair. **[fig. 57]**

Just as during the days of the Roman Empire it was said, "All roads lead to Rome," in 1934 Greyhound declared, "All Greyhound Routes Lead to Chicago World's Fair." In this *Saturday Evening Post* advertisement from May 26, 1934, Greyhound reminded travelers that for the Fair's second season, "again the gates swing open to a spectacle of amazing splendor, to a carnival of color and light, to countless features of science and art that startle the imagination." Greyhound Lines offered both "direct scenic travel to Chicago [and] the only automotive transportation within the Fair Grounds…fast express service, or leisurely sightseeing tours, in streamlined

Fig. 57. *GBM*

Fig. 58. *GBM*

coaches as modern as the Exposition." Greyhound assured the traveler that the trip to the Fair would be "a long-remembered journey, over highways famous for scenic, historic charm." **[fig. 58]**

Advertising also contributed to persuading the traveling public that appearance and style mattered and buses must be up to date, look "modern," and be an essential requirement to enjoy the romance of the road. This advertisement offers an invitation to "Ride with Greyhound down the beautiful Main Streets of America." Each "Main Street" features a newly restyled Yellow Coach bus, part of the display of the "charm and beauty of America!" **[fig. 59]** "*This year*, Find out for Yourself why millions have turned to Greyhound for First Class travel at far less cost." Prominently featured, a newly restyled Yellow Coach bus promises the open-minded (and who would want to be otherwise) something "new and modern." Acknowledging that ten or fifteen years ago "a bus trip was often an ordeal," the advertisement asserts it was time to "Try Greyhound now, *this year!*" The "big comfortable coaches" provided adjustable "deeply-cushioned chairs" permitting "comfortable relaxation or sleep." **[fig. 60]**

Fig. 59. *GBM*

Fig. 60. *GBM*

Fig. 61. *GBM*

Holiday travel offered opportunities for increased Greyhound ridership. Iconic images abound in this advertisement. **[fig. 61]** With the United States as a backdrop there is Santa Claus as well as all the "trimmings" for the holidays. Dancing couples and an hourglass suggest New Year's celebrations. A tree branch, lights and decorations; a turkey; a joyful shopper laden with wrapped gifts; a doll for that special child; and the star remind the reader of the birth of Christ and Christmas. Of course the newest Yellow Coach Greyhound bus is included. "Holiday happiness follows highways that lead home!" declares this advertisement. "The most heart-warming traditions of our land center around home-coming at Christmas and the New Year. The romance that has always clung highway travel returns in double measure with this year's trips by Greyhound." **[fig. 62]**

Despite the significant financial impact of the Great Depression, the ability to attract and keep customers also depended on Greyhound's ability to respond to the most common complaints about bus travel—an uncomfortable bus, so-called "greasy" lunch counters, and "filthy toilets at rest stops." Women, who

Fig. 62. *GBM*

Fig. 63. 1933 Nite Coach. *AACA*

made up about 60 percent of Greyhound's passengers, most often made these complaints. Greyhound's advertising, often focusing on women, reflected these concerns. *Fortune* identified Greyhound's response, noting, "Greyhound has spent lavishly to reduce bus discomfort."

Part of this "lavish" spending included the purchase of new buses offering improved passenger comfort. This included a 1933 version of the Nite Coach, originally introduced in 1928. It featured single and double berths with curtains and drapes to divide compartments, radios in each compartment, a men's and women's lavatory, a women's lounge with a mirror and dressing table, and a side aisle providing access to all compartments. Berths included mirrors and "wash basins" with hot and cold running water. While a compartment-based sleeper, this Nite Coach included some features appearing on future Greyhound buses. It offered inside storage of luggage below the passenger compartment as well as below the elevated driver's compartment accessible through the grille-door. A rear-mounted engine powered the bus that was also equipped with front and rear Westinghouse air brakes. A microphone in the engine bay allowed the driver to monitor "motor operation." In particular, the overall silhouette reflects the design of the 1935 X-1 and its successors. The basic configuration of the motor coach of today reflects this Night Coach design. **[fig. 63]**

In 1934, Greyhound displayed a Nite Coach for inspection by moviegoers attending San Francisco's Orpheum to watch *Cross Country Cruise.* Starring Lew Ayres, June Knight, Alice White, and Alan Dinehart, the film featured Greyhound buses. The theater also took the occasion to modify the box office to reflect parlor coach bus design. **[fig. 64]** While few remember this film, another has become

Publicity photograph of a Nite Coach compartment arranged for day travel (top). The compartment made up for night travel. *GBM*

legendary. In its August 1934 issue, *Fortune*, acknowledging the status of the Greyhound bus, even made it a co-star. "A great-granddaughter of the Hup, by now so entrenched in the transportation world and the popular mind that it was chosen to play opposite Clark Gable in his heroic venture, *It Happened One Night.*" While Gable traveled on a Greyhound bus, Claudette Colbert, left out in this description, provided the essential traveling partner in the love story that gave an added dimension to the notion of "the romance of the road."

Greyhound continued to purchase parlor coach models, but the buses no longer featured the rear end styling reflecting railroad observation cars. **[fig. 65]** On location at the Cleveland Art Museum, this

Fig. 64. San Francisco, California, 1934. *AACA*

Fig. 65. Yellow Coach Model 788. *AACA*

Fig. 66. Yellow Coach Model 788. *GBM*

33-passenger Yellow Coach Model 788 features a 1934 World's Fair, Chicago, Travel by Greyhound Lines advertisement. Yellow Coach sales brochures promoted the new "pleasingly streamlined" styling. While altered significantly from earlier parlor observation buses, the Model 788 continued to feature steps and ladders for access to luggage storage on the roof. **[fig. 66]**

Greyhound also added other Yellow Coach models. Shown on San Francisco's waterfront in 1935 is a parlor coach "Type 250" Model 843. **[fig. 67]** Yellow Coach first introduced the "Type 250 Coaches" in 1930 with parlor coach bodies incorporating railroad observation car features. Yellow Coach sales brochures emphasized the new styling and the retention of the original basic engineering design and chassis construction of the Type 250. Recognizing the limitations inherent in the nation's "work in progress" highway system, Yellow noted the "engine is entirely dual. Dual type carburetor, dual ignition, dual fuel pump, dual fan belts, dual spark plugs—operate together or independent of each other, and provide positive insurance against road delays." **[fig. 68]** A view of the 1936 Model 843's interior.

This advertisement, from *The Highway Traveler*, June/July 1936, features the more streamlined parlor coach. Offering a portrayal of aspiration, it compares travel in a "modern Greyhound bus" to the "sweep of a gull through sea-scented air." The advertisement further declares, "No transportation in the land offers quite so enjoyable way to reach any chosen vacation spot—and certainly no other offers so many miles for so few dollars." The romantic appeal of a vacation at the ocean attractively illustrated in the artist's modernistic depiction needs to be set against the reality of a nation still emerging from the Great Depression. **[fig. 69]**

While not a significant portion of its fleet, Grey-

Fig. 67. Yellow Coach Type 250 Model 843. San Francisco, California, 1935. *AACA*

Fig. 67. Yellow Coach Type 250 Model 843. *AACA*

Fig. 68. Yellow Coach Model 843 interior. *AACA*

Fig. 69. *GBM*

hound continued to purchase White and A.C.F. buses. This 1934 White Model 54A 29-passenger parlor coach features a visibly prominent revision of the railroad-inspired observation car of earlier parlor car buses. **[fig. 70]** The styling of this A.C.F. Model H-9-P represents a considerable departure from the earlier A.C.F. parlor coaches purchased by Greyhound in the 1920s. The bus features bi-fold entrance doors used on "Street Car Type" coach bodies for city, rather than intercity, service. A six-cylinder Hall-Scott engine mounted under the passenger floor powered the bus. **[fig 71]** These photographs provide interior views of the Model H-9-P. **[fig. 72, 73]**

These restyled buses were part of the larger effort to develop visionary responses to the Great Depression. In his book, *Twentieth Century Limited*, Jeffrey Meikle noted, "Industrial designers have always considered their profession a 'depression baby.'" As a result of the economic collapse, manufacturers of products as diverse as pencil sharpeners, refrigerators, tractors, automobiles, trucks, and buses hoping to survive "turned to radical solutions because they had nothing to lose; to the optimistic or the desperate such solutions seemed a panacea." As a solution, designers promised a distinctive product, providing designs that would produce a signature "look" for a company seeking to set itself apart from the rest. New styling made the older parlor coach designs look obsolete.

Fig. 70. 1934 White Model 54A. *AACA*

Fig. 71. A.C.F. Model H-9-P. *AACA*

Fig. 72. A.C.F. Model H-9-P interior. *AACA*

Fig. 73. A.C.F. Model H-9-P interior. *AACA*

Accepting the viability of utilizing design to increase ticket sales and income, Greyhound assumed leadership for the development of a radically different bus. The bus offered travelers a new streamlined ride, a literal embodiment of the utopian visions offering an optimistic view of the future. For the Greyhound traveler, the future was the present. In 1935, Greyhound unveiled the X-1, placing it in service between Chicago and Detroit. Greyhound publicity proclaimed the bus was "as new as tomorrow" and "as far ahead of current matters as next year's calendar." The experimental bus developed by the Yellow Coach Division of General Motors Truck Company and Greyhound became the basis for the 1936 Yellow Coach Model 719, referred to as the Super-Coach by Greyhound. The new coach clearly reflected the commitment to utilizing design and style to offer a "streamlined" and "modernistic" product to encourage increased travel. **[fig. 74]** It remains *the* template for motor coach design.

Fig. 74. Greyhound X-1. *AACA*

Readers of *Bus Transportation*, June 1935, learned about the X-1 in an article entitled "Unleashing the Super Greyhound." Despite assertions that the X-1's were "an experiment pure and simple," their design boldly represented the shape of things to come. Relying on Greyhound and Yellow Coach/General Motors publicity material, *Bus Transportation* declared, "these coaches embody every modern improvement for passenger comfort—improved riding qualities, better visibility, better ventilation and many other innovations which point to an entirely new trend in intercity coach design. Conservatively streamlined, they offer eye-arresting appeal in the Greyhound colors of blue and white with gold striping and lettering." **[fig. 75]**

Fig. 75. Greyhound X-1. *GBM*

Fig. 76. Greyhound X-1. *AACA*

The X-1 represented significant, even revolutionary, departures from even the newly restyled parlor coach buses added to Greyhound's fleet. *Bus Transportation* noted, "One of the most unique features of these new coaches is the elevated seating arrangement which places passengers above the dust, noise and vibration level, permitting them to look directly out over traffic. The interior of the body is completely free of all obstructions and is given over entirely to passenger use." In addition, "the seats are elevated to a point higher than the wheels, thereby eliminating uncomfortable wheelhouse seats and facing all 36 passengers forward." Following the wording of Greyhound publicity, readers learned that appearances could possibly be deceiving. "From first appearance it seems that these new coaches are much higher than present day coaches. However, this is not the case. In fact they are two inches lower than the coaches now being operated by the Greyhound Lines, and have a center of gravity lower than other existing equipment." Since existing Greyhound buses provided seats for 33 passengers, the X-1 promised greater passenger revenues by providing seating for three additional passengers. An earlier proposal provided only 34 seats. **[fig. 76]**

According to Greyhound, the "pleasing and restful" interior followed "modernistic lines." The "deeply upholstered in mohair" reclining seats "of modern design" featuring magnesium and aluminum alloy construction were "1/3 lighter than other coach seats and equally as strong." A "tubular diffusing lens running entirely around the sides and end of the coach above the passengers' heads, and also down the center of the roof over the recessed aisle" lit the interior. Ventilation in the pre-air conditioning days featured four ducts that ran lengthwise between the inside and outside roof panels with two to intake fresh air and two for exhausting air from the coach. Fresh air entered from vents above the windshield and entered the interior through "slotted moulding over the side windows." Four "double unit heaters" and one for the front vestibule and driver compartment supplied heat for the interior. The photograph of the production Model 719 Super-Coach, shown below, features interiors virtually identical to the X-1.

Clay models and drawings provide insights into the design process. This stylist's clay model reflects the essential features of the final version of the X-1. **[fig. 77]** These scale models provide stylists with opportunities to judge the design in three dimen-

Fig. 77. Greyhound X-1.design. *AACA*

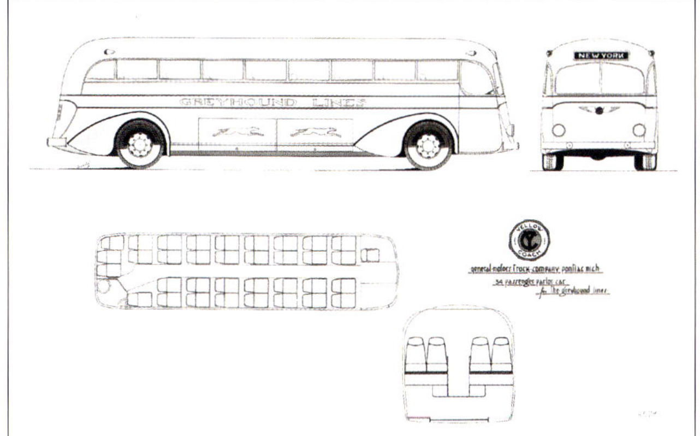

Fig. 78. Greyhound X-1.design. *MBS*

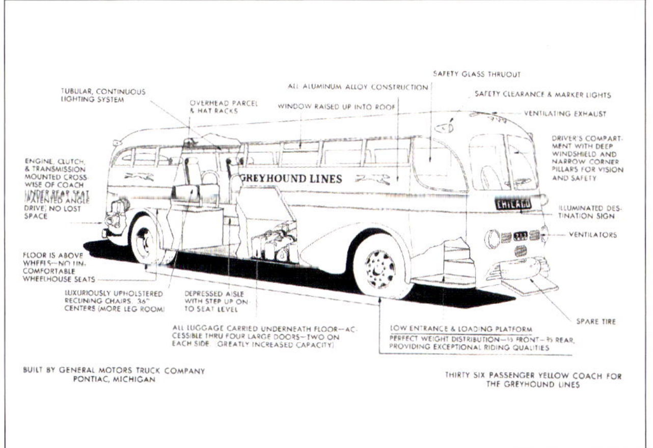

Fig. 79. Greyhound X-1.design. *MBS*

Fig. 80. Greyhound X-1. *MBS*

sions and thus more realistically assess a design's proportions. The artist's illustrations of the exterior from Yellow Coach use the long-established "Parlor car" to refer to the body style. The 34-passenger design includes a lavatory. **[fig. 78]** This illustration shows modifications to the original design. No longer equipped with a lavatory, the bus accommodated 36 passengers. **[fig. 79]**

In another radical departure from parlor coach design, the X-1 featured a transversely mounted rear engine located under the rear seats. This allowed for a very different design, eliminating the hood and the extra length of a front-mounted engine design. The bus also featured two "large water tight and dust proof" baggage compartments eliminating the necessity to store baggage vulnerable to the elements in a roof rack. Interior baggage racks offered space for "parcels and wraps." These features more than doubled the baggage capacity of existing Greyhound buses.

Bus Transportation and, in particular, the *Aluminum News-Letter* made much of the "aluminum alloys which were used throughout as the principal materials of construction." This resulted in a "perfectly balanced vehicle" with "great structural strength" while "reducing the weight of the vehicle more than 2 tons from the present Greyhound coaches." The design promised style with savings—the lighter weight meant better fuel mileage and possibly greater longevity for structural as well as mechanical components. **[fig. 80]** The *Aluminum News-Letter* also featured a Greyhound publicity photograph illustrat-

Fig. 81. Greyhound X-1 testing. *MBS*

Fig. 82. Greyhound X-1 testing. *AACA*

ing passenger loading probably designed to dispel notions that the elevated passenger area would prove awkward for passengers. The riveted construction of the bus is apparent. **[fig. 81]**

Greyhound developed two additional experimental models, the X-2 and X-3. The X-2, placed in service between Chicago and Pittsburgh, featured front-end modifications more in line with the production Super-Coach. Reports indicate that like the X-1 shown during actual test service **[fig. 82]**, the X-3 saw test service between Chicago and Detroit.

These experimental models paved the way for the introduction of the Yellow Coach Model 719, Greyhound's Super-Coach. Underscoring the rapidity of Super-Coach development following the public introduction and test service announcement for the X-1 in June 1935, is this October 11, 1935 General Motors Art and Colour Section stylist's rendering that clearly resembles the production version. **[fig. 83]**

Fig. 83. Yellow Coach Model 719 deisgn study. *AACA*

"Triumph In Motor Bus Design." The headline heralded the debut of the Yellow Coach Model 719. "THERE SHE ROLLS—*the new Greyhound Super-Coach—a streamlined symphony in blue and white! She takes the hills as easily as a sixteen-cylinder roadster—rides as steadily as a modern ocean liner.*" Superlatives were the order of the day for Greyhound's advertisement introducing the Model 719 Super-Coach. Despite the advertising hyperbole the new bus offered significant and even revolutionary design features. The Model 719 Super-Coach offered a revised front end and vents at the rear engine compartment while retaining nearly all of the features of the startling X-1 introduced in June 1935. The advertisement continued: "This is truly a triumph in motor bus design. Greyhound, world-leader in long distance bus transportation, wanted an ultra-modern passenger vehicle .... It was a job for master builders. So General Motors Truck Company...was commissioned to do the job. Differing as widely from present buses as night from day, this new Super-Coach heralds a bright new era in highway travel—puts it right up in front of any transportation—land, sea, or air! The first ride will convince you." **[fig. 84]**

Greyhound published a folder in 1936 providing details about the new Model 719 declaring, "*Step inside* Greyhound's New Super Coach! The Last Word in *Modern Highway Travel* [...]. As the next best thing to an actual trip in the Super-Coach, take this 'conducted tour' through the new Greyhound." The folder highlighted twelve features focusing on passenger comfort. "The seat deck is higher—well above the wheel housings, above the vibration line, above the noise and fumes of traffic." The depressed aisle allows the passenger to "walk upright" in the

Fig. 84. Model 719 Super-Coach. *AACA*

bus. The "luxurious chairs recline in four different positions" and as the passengers "stretch out and enjoy the trip" they also have an adjustable "rubber-roller type of footrest" to add to their comfort. The windows featured "roll-down smartly designed aluminum shades similar to Venetian blinds." Frosted glass tubing provided light "bright enough to read by—yet gentle enough not to disturb sleep." The "streamlined" overhead rack provided easy access to small parcels and wraps. **[fig. 85]**

Aspects of the overall design of the Super-Coach were also among the twelve highlighted features. The "extra-deep windshield gives your driver at all times an unusually good view of the road ahead." The "curb-level step and the additional step and a half up to the depressed aisle," eliminated having passengers "climb" into the bus. "Baggage is locked below decks" so that "passengers have the coach to themselves." **[fig. 86]** The "motor rides behind," resulting in "less noise, less vibration, smoother operation, and a complete lack of exhaust fumes."

Automobile Topics covered the Super-Coach introduction in its August 17, 1936 issue claiming it "One of the most significant developments in motor bus transportation." The article offered this analysis: "In a way, the 'Super-Coach' is the answer to the challenge which is contained in the railroads' development of the streamlined, light-weight Diesel-driven trains [...]. Greyhound's new coach represents a new conception of design [...]. This new Super-Coach is a blunt-nosed, modernistic vehicle in the familiar blue-and-white Greyhound colors, with glittering metal trim. It is not streamlined to exaggeration, but has

Fig. 85. Model 719 Super-Coach interior. *GBM*

Fig. 86. Model 719 Super-Coach. *HML*

smooth and flowing contours that instantly impress observers with a feeling of fleetness and power." The reference to exaggerated streamlining probably reflected the author's view of the Chrysler and DeSoto Airflow models introduced in 1934. **[fig. 87]**

Travelers could visit three major expositions in 1936. The Texas Centennial at Dallas, the Great Lakes Exposition celebrating Cleveland, Ohio's hundredth birthday, and the California Pacific International Exposition, held in Balboa Park, San Diego. This *Saturday Evening Post* advertisement promoted them as "A magnificent three-ring performance—in three great states." Greyhound recalled a child's capacity to wonder. "Remember childhood days, when you went google-eyed with joy and wonder as you gazed at a radiant circus poster, promising 'The

Fig. 87. Model 719 Super-Coach. *MBS*

Fig. 88. *GBM*

Greatest Show on Earth'?" But Greyhound wanted more than child-like responses. After all, adults spent the money to travel. "This year, that promise will come true in a larger way than childish fancy ever pictured! In three great cities, three world expositions will be in full swing, offering the most fascinating three-ring show in American history." Greyhound offered travelers the opportunity to visit one or all three "by a Greyhound circle tour." **[fig. 88]**

Greyhound selected a 1936 White Model 704-T tractor, manufactured by the Cleveland-based White Motor Company, for the Great Lakes Exposition tractor-trailer unit. Unlike the General Motors vehicles at A Century of Progress in Chicago, the cab received no streamline styling modifications, with the exception of skirting to hide the rear wheels. The Bender Body Company, also of Cleveland, manufactured the 45-passenger trailers. **[fig. 89]**

This photograph features the Greyhound exhibit at the 1935-1936 California Pacific International Exposition, in San Diego. President Franklin D. Roosevelt and First Lady Eleanor visited the Exposition during the first year. Over 7,200,000 visitors took in the Exposition during its two-year run. In

Fig. 89. 1936 White Model 704-T. *AACA*

Fig. 90. California Pacific International Exposition, 1936. *AACA*

Fig. 91. General Motors design study, 1936. *MBS*

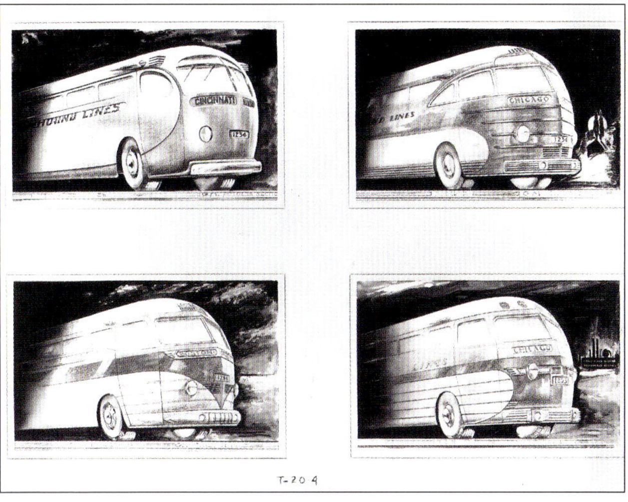

Fig. 92. General Motors design study, 1936. *MBS*

addition to buildings that reflected the modernist aesthetic, the Exposition used the Spanish-Colonial Revival Style buildings that remained from the 1915-1916 Panama-Pacific Exposition. **[fig. 90]**

Meanwhile, the General Motors Art and Colour Section continued development of designs for future buses. A series of stylist's renderings indicates a direction General Motors' production buses did not take. The rendering by P. Zampol, dated June 17, 1936, **[fig. 91]** illustrates the emphasis on a streamlined, rounded, elongated teardrop shape. Of the designs shown in the collection of four renderings, three—dated June 18, 22, and 26, 1936—feature a rounded front end with a clearly defined center crease, while one design—dated August 30, 1936—offers a smooth rounded surface. **[fig. 92]** Often identified as a scale clay model of the Model 719, the photograph dated September 25, 1936, actually illustrates possible revisions or alternatives to the Super-Coach.

Fig. 93. General Motors design study, 1936. *MBS*

Fig. 94. General Motors design study, 1937. *MBS*

[**fig. 93**] The somewhat more rounded nose and tail reflects aspects of designs offered in the renderings developed months earlier. The February 26, 1937 rendering [**fig. 94**] continues to illustrate the streamlined teardrop shape. Whether the design features a smooth or creased nose is unclear due to the side view profile rendering. They do reflect the design of buses manufactured by Flxible and purchased by Greyhound, such as the Clipper Model 25 introduced in 1938. [**fig. 95**] Greyhound also purchased buses with bodies mounted on truck chassis that offered the teardrop shape. The 1936 Flxible Airway with a Chevrolet chassis is an example. [**fig 96**] In 1913, Hugo H. Young founded the Flexible Side Car Company in Loudonville, Ohio, to manufacture a patented motorcycle sidecar with a wheel that would stay on the ground as the motorcycle took a curve. The sidecar also attached to the motorcycle with a "flexible" connection, hence the company's name. In 1919, company directors dropped the first "e" creating the Flxible Company. When the price of a Model T dropped to less than the cost of a motorcycle and sidecar in 1920, Flxible shifted production to funeral cars, ambulances, and buses. Prior to 1936, most Flxible buses featured bodies mounted on Buick chassis.

Acting conservatively, Greyhound's Yellow Coach Model 743 Super-Coach, introduced in 1937, continued the styling established by the first Super-Coach with only minor changes. The decorative parts that are on either side of the destination window are ver-

Fig. 95. 1938 Flxible Clipper Model 25. *GBM*

Fig. 96. 1937 Flxible Airway. *GBM*

Fig. 97. Yellow Coach Model 743. *AACA*

Fig. 98. Yellow Coach Model 743. *AACA*

tical on the Model 719 and horizontal with built-in turn signals on the Model 743. The bezels surrounding the headlights feature three groups of three horizontal bars below the headlights on the Model 719, while there is only one grouping of three bars on the Model 743. **[fig. 97]**

In other styling changes, the Model 743 featured revised rear end grillwork and only two windows. Still in service, an early version undergoing engine maintenance in Roanoke, Virginia, features a 1940 World's Fair logo. Housing enclosed the rear marker lights—other examples do not. **[fig. 98]** Later versions of the Model 743 featured air conditioning. The installation included the compressor unit under the passenger deck and the blower and evaporator above the rear windows. Visible on these models are ventilation grills above the next to last side windows and on the sides of the bus. **[fig. 99]**

Fig. 99. Yellow Coach Model 743. *AACA*

Greyhound developed the Model 745, based on the Model 719 and 743, indicating it considered the reintroduction of sleeper service. **[fig. 100]** Noticeable is the heightened roof area. As the interior views illustrate, sleeping berths occupied the space above the passenger seats, necessitating the high roof. **[fig. 101]** Greyhound produced only one of these models intended to seat thirty and sleep twenty.

Just as Greyhound utilized visionary styling for radically different buses, it also sought to develop a complementary architectural style for its terminals, thus creating a harmonious corporate aesthetic. Prominent in this effort was William Sudwick Arrasmith, the architect responsible for the design of over 35 Greyhound bus terminals in the 1930s and 1940s. In his study of Arrasmith in *The Streamline Era Greyhound Terminals*, Frank E. Wrenick argues, "The year 1937 was a pivotal one for Greyhound. The company had finally implemented its program to create a new corporate image, integrating architectural and vehicle designs, and commenced a massive program of building terminals that would be under its exclusive control and suit its needs." Wrenick's choice of 1937 coincides with the introduction of the Super-Coach and the opening of Arrasmith's first Greyhound commission, the Louisville, Kentucky, terminal in that year. "Thus in 1937, for the first time ever, buses and their terminals were unified in design, appearance and efficiency. A Super Coach bus parked next to a streamline Greyhound Blue ter-

Fig. 100. Yellow Coach Model 7435. *AACA*

minal projected an impression of cohesiveness that could not have helped but make a favorable impression on the clientele, while the comfort and efficiency of the terminal mirrored that of the coaches. This gave the passengers the feeling that they had actually begun their journey once they approached one of Arrasmith's new porcelain paneled terminals."

Greyhound's program to develop its corporate image reflected the culture-wide effort to promote modernism in industrial and architectural design. "Streamline Moderne," the label used by Wrenick to refer to the Greyhound architectural aesthetic, is one of a number of labels including "WPA Modern"—for public buildings designed for the New Deal's Works Progress Administration and Public Works Administration—and "Depression Modern." These various labels reflect variations within the larger modernist movement—a more all-encompassing label. The essential motifs of Streamline Moderne include an emphasis on horizontality, extended bands of windows, rounded corners, and minimal decoration. Overall, Greyhound terminals constructed in the 1930s and 1940s, while incorporating the basic elements of Streamline Moderne design, feature numerous variations and departures reflective of the larger modernist movement.

Fig. 101. Yellow Coach Model 745 interior. *GBM*

Fig. 102. *GBM*

Fig. 103. *GBM*

Fig. 104. Greyhound depot, 34th Street, New York. *AACA*

This 1937 *Saturday Evening Post* advertisement illustrates Greyhound's effort to pair both the Super-Coach and the terminal—based on the design for Minneapolis—to illustrate design "cohesiveness" as a crucial element in travel. Both represent "Portals to Pleasant Trips!" The traveler first "passes through" the terminal doorway and then boards the bus. The result is travel that offers the romance of the road. "For a brand new world exists on the other side... one that is filled with changing scenes, interesting people, new experiences—a swift-moving panorama of America on parade." **[fig. 102]**

Wrenick does acknowledge that, "Streamline styling was not new to Greyhound before Arrasmith designed the 1937 Louisville terminal." Extending this argument further he asserts, "No attempt was ever made before to cover a structure of any size in colored porcelain enamel panels, and certainly never using such a dramatic color scheme as Greyhound Blue." However, Greyhound advertising illustrates the use of blue porcelain panels prior to 1937. This 1935 advertisement features "one of three modern terminals at the heart of New York City." **[fig. 103]** The July 1935 issue of *Bus Transportation* also suggests the effort to develop a unique corporate aesthetic predated 1937. Describing the New York terminal featured in the advertisement, the article noted, "It is a two-story building of distinctive Greyhound design, encased with blue tile and chromium trimmings." Supporting part of Wrenick's argument, this photograph of the terminal indicates the entire building was not "encased with blue tile." **[fig. 104]**

Greyhound Terminal Album: 1930s

Beaumont, Texas. *AACA*

Hollywood, California. *AACA*

Palatka, Florida. *AACA*

Binghamton, New York. *AACA*

Los Angeles, California. *AACA*

Sacramento, California. *AACA*

Eugene, Oregon. *AACA*

Minneapolis, Minnesota. *AACA*

Savannah, Georgia. *AACA*

Long Beach, California. *AACA*

Omaha, Nebraska. *AACA*

Spokane, Washington. *AACA*

Toledo, Ohio. *GBM*

Detroit, Michigan. *GBM*

Colorado Springs, Colorado. *AACA*

St. Petersburg, Florida. *AACA*

Albuquerque, New Mexico. *AACA*

San Luis Obispo, California. *AACA*

The Super-Coach was on prominent display in Greyhound advertising. In the April/May 1937 issue of *The Highway Traveler* it is the star attraction as it flies along a rural highway while a Robin perches on a branch. The advertisement features key elements of travel. First, what you will see along the way. "It is natural for a Greyhound advertisement to talk about Spring—because only Greyhound travel (following the great main highways of America) is chummy with the first pink and green flush of the new season…intimate with bursting buds, fresh-turned furrows, early song birds. Is it any wonder that millions of travelers who thrill to natural beauty are planning Spring trips by Greyhound?" Second, how you will travel—the comfort of the bus. The "new Super-Coaches (or 'Cruisers') [are] writing a new chapter in highway travel. Passengers say they are quite above comparison, for smooth, gliding ride, deep cushioned comfort […]. Cozy armchairs […]." Third is the cost. "[N]o Spring in travel history has seen such low ticket cost per mile." **[fig. 105]**

Fig. 105. *GBM*

The Highway Traveler, October/November 1937, featured this advertisement depicting the boarding of a Super-Coach. The festive scene features a well-dressed white middle class crowd. Value is the theme. "For Sale America's Smartest, Smoothest Travel. Terms: No down payment, nothing per month, garage and upkeep free. All you pay is 1/3 the cost of driving a small private car." The bus is a desirable alternative to the "family auto" for vacation trips. It's "a smooth-rolling land cruiser that can't be matched in riding ease by the swankiest limousine ever built—one which will give your automobile and yourself a welcome rest—will help you to relax and enjoy the intimate beauty of all outdoors, while saving dollars on every trip." Safety and security a concern? You also got the services of a "smartly uniformed, expert driver, who holds the finest safety record in America." Four social tableaux suggest how to "Enjoy Autumn's fleeting glory." **[fig. 106]**

Fig. 106. *GBM*

Greyhound utilized women in a variety of guises in its advertising featuring the Super-Coach. An artist's illustration of an attractive swimsuit-attired young woman dominates this advertisement and successfully gets in all probability the male reader's attention. The much smaller Greyhound Super-Coach illustration stands in sharp contrast. Ostensibly appealing to the value-conscious female traveler, *The Highway Traveler*, December 1936/January 1937

Fig. 107. *MBS*

Fig. 108. *MBS*

advertisement declares "Picture yourself soaking up health-giving sunshine at a gay Florida resort—while Old Man Winter grips all the North! Not for me, you sigh. Such vacations are for millionaires. Don't ever believe it! That old barrier of expense is down—leveled by the balloon tires of a thousand Greyhound buses, bound for health and sunshine." Combining appeals to glamour with practical considerations of cost and safety, men might picture meeting attractive women should they travel. **[fig. 107]**

"Smart Smooth Cool! And their cost is lowest of all." Ostensibly describing the "Greyhound Super-Coach Vacations," the leggy young woman draped across the advertisement most likely attracts the reader's immediate attention, as she certainly seems smart, smooth, and cool! Does sex appeal sell? Now that Greyhound has your attention take note of the variety of vacations and then "See a brand new America this summer—one you scarcely knew existed!" Do you need more facts? Clip the coupon in this advertisement from the June/July 1938 issue of *The Highway Traveler*, check the booklets you want, mail it in and soon you will have what you need to plan your Super-Coach vacation." **[fig. 108]**

"Picture *yourself* having fun on a Greyhound trip." The independent young woman traveling on a Greyhound Super-Coach is having fun. For some reason, "up pops old Chief Ump-Ump-Wah," and snaps her picture as she is taking his. Reflecting prevailing stereotypes, the advertisement seen in *The Highway Traveler*, April/May 1938 considers this an example of "thrilling surprises" offered by a Greyhound bus trip. Such trips offer "unique and pleasant incidents that you don't seem to find, traveling any other way." Expect to save since fares are "25% to 65% lower than rates for other types of travel." **[fig. 109]**

In December 1937, *Collier's* readers were encouraged to "Laugh at Old Man Winter!" Young women could do this in two ways. One option: "Travel South to Sunshine" traveling to "gay Florida beaches," or "along the warm Gulf Coast, through the romantic southwest, or in colorful California." The other option: "North to Holiday Fun!" enjoying "happy reunions with family and friends." Reflecting recurring themes, the advertisement pledged the trip would be "with congenial fellow passengers" and "will be warm, safe, scenic." **[fig. 110]**

"This can happen to YOU!" This colorful advertisement from *The Highway Traveler* December1938/

Fig. 109. *MBS*

Fig. 110. *GBM*

January 1939, offers seven social tableaux for dreaming. The target is the resident of the North, a young woman in particular, or men who would like to meet a woman like this. Travel can be about *that kind* of romance as well as the romance that means adventure. "When Winter whips the North, how would you like to sprawl on shining sand, near sounding surf—while a southern sun paints you a golden tan?" This inviting word picture accompanies the illustration of an attractive young woman working on her "golden tan." **[fig. 111]**

By the late 1930s, the Great Depression still lingered. The so-called "Roosevelt Depression" of 1938 saw automobile and truck production decline by over 50 percent with unemployment levels close to early depression levels. This reminded everyone that "the stormy weather of the economic hurricane" remained. A new "storm" loomed as well. The Japanese had invaded Manchuria in 1931 and China in 1937. Mussolini's Italy had invaded Ethiopia in 1935. Following Hitler's rise to power in Germany in 1933, a series of expansionist actions including the annexation of Austria in 1938, the occupation of Czecho-

Fig. 111. *MBS*

slovakia in early 1939, and Germany's invasion of Poland on September 1, 1939, resulted in a declaration of war against Germany by England and France on September 3rd, the official start of World War II.

The New York World's Fair began as these new "storm" clouds gathered. David Gelernter in *1939: The Lost World of the Fair* argues the Fair offered a window onto the culture of the 1930s. "To understand the United States of America in the late 1930s, you have no choice. You must see the fair. In that small slice of time and space, the city and its vast visiting crowds enjoyed what might be the best gift of all—to glimpse and yet not possess the Promised Land." In particular, "Fairgoers at the most popular exhibit on the grounds, General Motors' Futurama, were addressed from 'the future' by a deep portentous voice: 'Man has forged ahead.... New and better things have sprung from his industry and genius.'" Greyhound offered this advertisement to entice the traveler. Reflecting utopian dreams of the future, it offers a social tableau of a well-dressed middle class American family about to enter the Fair where "an incredible dream city comes to life, stretching for miles in the fantastic designs of tomorrow's architecture, glowing with futuristic murals." **[fig. 112]**

Fig. 112. *MBS*

Planning and development for the New York World's Fair began in the first half of the 1930s. President Franklin Delano Roosevelt officially dedicated the opening of the Fair on April 30, 1939. First day attendance totaled approximately 400,000 with a total first year attendance of 26 million. Closing on October 31, 1939, the Fair reopened May 11, 1940. 19 million visitors took in the Fair in its second year for a total of 45 million visitors. In its two-year run, A Century of Progress had totaled 38 million visitors. Once again, Greyhound sought to tap this huge potential market, offering travelers an affordable, comfortable, and convenient means to travel to the Fair. As it did in Chicago and Cleveland, Greyhound also offered transportation inside the New York World's Fair in specially designed vehicles.

Automobile Topics, July 25, 1938, provided details. "The largest buses in the world are to be used on the grounds of the New York World's Fair 1939, it was announced last week at the time of signing a contract with Greyhound Corp. for their operation. The buses, 100 in number, to be built by Yellow Truck & Coach, will be 45 feet long and 9 feet wide, with a capacity of 120 persons. Standard buses are 33 by 8 feet. Raymond Loewy, well known industrial designer, styled the buses." The article noted, "The fair's buses are expected to carry 30,000,000 people over the 10 miles of roads on the grounds. Fare of 10 cents will be collected at stations so that one-man operation will be possible." **[fig. 113]**

Automobile Topics continued: "Ralph Bogan, assistant to the president of the Greyhound Corp. and president of Exposition Greyhound Lines, the organization created to operate Greyhound's World's Fair fleet, said that the buses would be streamlined to express the forward-looking theme of the Fair with bodies slung lower than on standard makes. They will be of the pusher type with engines in the rear, and special precautions are being taken to prevent the odor of exhaust fumes from annoying passengers and pedestrians."

As with other expositions, the three and a half mile long, and up to a mile wide 1,216.5-acre New York World's Fair offered utopian visions. One vision forecast days made up of eight hours of work, eight hours of rest, eight hours of leisure. Reflecting the

Fig. 113. New York World's Fair bus, 1939. *AACA*

Fig. 114. World's Fair "sidewalk crawler." *AACA*

THE FAIR'S THEME EXHIBIT

A **MAGIC** carpet ride through space "two miles" above a perfectly integrated garden city of tomorrow features the central theme exhibit of the New York World's Fair.

The theme exhibit is housed in the eighteen story Perisphere, companion piece to the 700-foot Trylon, both of which together constitute the architectural focus of the Fair.

The entrance to the theme exhibit is high up on the side of the Perisphere fifty feet above the ground. Access is by means of the two longest moving stairways ever built in this country. Visitors enter on two levels and step on to two magic carpets placed one above the other and moving in opposite directions. These carpets or platforms form huge rings seemingly unsupported in space which slowly revolve, carrying spectators around the sphere to exit bridges leading down the helicline.

Spectators entering at the beginning of a cycle see a daylight panorama spread out beneath them and stretching off to the horizon on all sides. Clouds form patterns overhead, and their shadows are seen passing over the countryside beneath. Soft music is heard.

The 700-foot three-sided Trylon and the 200-foot Perisphere are the dominant architectural features of the New York World's Fair. During the Fair the Trylon will be used as a beacon and also for broadcasting purposes. The Perisphere should prove one of the outstanding attractions of the 1939 show. Within it, from revolving platforms suspended in mid-air, visitors will view a dramatization of what has been called the "World of Tomorrow."

15

Fig. 115. *MBS*

Fair's 1939 motto, "Building the World of Tomorrow," the Focal Exhibit of the Production & Distribution Zone declared that at Washington's inauguration to "raise the incomes of the entire population to the Good Life Minimum would have been considered impossible. With modern technology and power production it is no longer physically impossible. We have the techniques and the power to produce abundance." In addition to the large buses, Greyhound operated forty "sidewalk crawlers"—three car and tractor trains designed for 36 passengers. The tractor, powered by an International truck engine, featured a modified International hood and grille assembly. **[fig. 114]**

Showcasing technology, the New York World's Fair offered examples of the latest in available technology and the utopian dreams of engineers and industrial designers. In *Twentieth Century Limited*, Jeffrey L. Meikle contends that Walter Dorwin Teague, designer of the Ford Motor Company pavilion and exhibit, "who served with six architects on the Board of Design, turned the fair's commercial promoters from an original intention to celebrate the 150th anniversary of Washington's inauguration as President at New York to a goal of envisioning the future society."

The most recognizable symbol of the Fair, the Trylon and Perisphere, represented the finite and the infinite, the present and the future. The Fair showcased the talents of Henry Dreyfuss, designer of the New York Central's 20th Century Limited Hudson J-3a locomotive and the 1938 Federal motor truck. In the Perisphere, his "Democracity," represented the 1939 utopian vision of the American city intended as a symbol of all city planning. This emphasis on planning resulted from the belief that *laissez faire* capitalism and the free market had failed and more centralized planning and control of the economy by government needed to occur. **[fig. 115]** This page from *The Highway Traveler*, April/May 1939, provides information about the Trylon and Perisphere, and Dreyfuss' exhibit featuring the "garden city of

Fig. 116. *MBS*

Fig. 117. *MBS*

tomorrow." **[fig. 116]** Visible in this advertisement from *The Highway Traveler*, August/September 1939 are key symbols of modernity: The Trylon and Perisphere, a Super-Coach, the unique bus used to travel at the Fair, and the jaunty couple. Greyhound also offered this folder to potential travelers to the World's Fair. **[fig 117]**

The General Motors' Futurama exhibit, the "hit of the fair" according to Meikle, designed by Norman Bel Geddes to represent America in 1960, was, Gelernter argues, "obsessed with cars" and even more importantly with roads, predicting an "elaborate infrastructure of control, modeled on the railroads." Given the sponsorship of General Motors this seems likely. However, Gelernter argues, once America built the superhighways, it stopped bothering with the elaborate control infrastructure Geddes imagined. This failure is part of the larger change in society. Meikle argues that after the war, "the Depression dream of building a harmonious machine age America dissolved." However, such a dream was one among many. Furthermore, the notion of "building a harmonious machine age" that would include an "elaborate infrastructure of control" was for most too all encompassing, too collectivist, requiring a nearly total transformation of society. During World War II, numerous utopian visions for the postwar world, including designs for postwar Greyhound buses developed by designer Raymond Loewy, tantalized the consumer. While hardly the "stuff" of highbrow dreams, many ordinary Americans saw these designs

Fig. 118. 1939 World's Fair exhibit. *AACA*

as tangible symbols of a future worth fighting for.

This scene feature Greyhound's 1939 Fair exhibit, its style the embodiment of the "modern" streamlined architecture of the Fair. Prominent is an air-conditioned Model 743 Super-Coach. Below the famous Greyhound logo, and reflecting the Fair's motto "Building the World of Tomorrow," is a display for "The Motor Coach of Tomorrow" featuring a large and dramatic artist's rendering of the next Super-Coach. Greyhound featured this new Super-Coach, later known as "Silversides," at the 1940 World's Fair. **[fig. 118]**

Fig. 119. 1940 World's Fair bus. *AACA*

Greyhound offered new graphics for its World's Fair buses in 1940. **[fig. 119]** This photograph offers an interesting view of Greyhound's bus, the umbrella-sheltered stand for fair-goers to purchase the 10-cent bus ride tickets, and clothing styles. The limited glimpse of the pavilions and grounds includes the spire of the Trylon at the right. **[fig. 120]**

In 1939, in addition to the World's Fair in New York, travelers had the opportunity to attend the Golden Gate International Exposition in San Francisco. Greyhound encouraged travelers to "Swing Around America! This Summer...by Greyhound" and visit both Fairs for $69.95. This price included "transportation from your home, across the continent to one fair, then back to the other, and return to your own home—following your choice of scenic routes." While the advertisement's emphasis was on value, the traveler got "fun, excitement and thrills." **[fig. 121]** This advertisement offers a romantic illustration of the Golden Gate International Exposition and the Greyhound Super-Coach—*the* "way to Trea-

Fig. 120. 1940 World's Fair bus. *AACA*

sure Island." **[fig. 122]** Greyhound offered this photograph, with dramatic searchlight beams, artfully added, to publicize the Exposition and Greyhound service. Greyhound's exhibit at the Exposition reflects the modernist elements prevalent in the architecture and design of the 1930s. **[fig. 123]**

Travel throughout the United States in the 1930s was often an adventure, but not in the romantic sense. While Greyhound advertisements promoted travel as romantic and exciting, more than half the United States highway system still remained "unimproved" by 1939. Improved did not necessarily mean a concrete, asphalt or other hard surface. Regularly maintained—that is graded and leveled—gravel and dirt roads were by 1930s standards labeled "improved." An example of a 1930s "improved" highway is on display in this photograph of a Model 743. While paved with concrete, the highway features two narrow unmarked lanes and narrow unpaved shoulders. Crossroads, shown in the distance, were common, creating potential accident sites. Traffic usually had to stop on only one of the roads, resulting in driver impatience as they coped with the difficulty of cross-

Fig. 121. *GBM*

Fig. 122. Golden Gate International Exposition. *AACA*

Fig. 123. Golden Gate International Exposition. *AACA*

ing or turning onto the through-road. **[fig. 124]**

In addition, travel by bus in the 1930s often necessitated frequent stops, usually every two hours. Intercity buses seldom featured on-board restroom facilities and consequently, in addition to the need to refuel and stop at regularly scheduled destinations, schedules accommodated stops for the convenience of passengers. *Fortune's* August 1934 article on Greyhound featured a color illustration of a roadside that accommodated buses—a filling station, "comfort station," stores, and a restaurant that sold food to the traveler. While hardly "romantic," this aspect of the travel experience along with the road and the final destinations became part of the "romance of the road." *Fortune* helped promote this image in the "Great American Roadside" in the September 1934 issue. While focusing on the automobile, the article also applied to travel by bus since the bus stopped at businesses that were part of the "Great American Roadside."

Fortune attributed the roadside to the ultimate source, declaring, "So God made the American restive" and this "restlessness of the American people" created the roadside. The story *Fortune* told featured five "characters:" the American continent; the American people; the automobile; the "Great American Road;" and the "Great American Roadside." The article asserted, "For only just now are people begin-

Fig. 124. Yellow Coach Model 743. *AACA*

ning to realize that these five characters, as they function in relation to one another, combine in simple fact to mean a new way of life, a new but powerfully established American institution." *Fortune* speculated "it may never have sharply occurred to you... that the 900,000 miles of hard-fleshed highway that this people has built—not just for transportation but to express something not well defined—is by very considerable odds the greatest road the human race has ever built. It may never have occurred to you that upon this continent and along this road this people casually moves in numbers and by distances which make the ancient and the grave migrations of Celt and Goth look like a smooth crossing on the Hoboken Ferry."

Offering descriptions of the "Great American Road," *Fortune's* account observed, "How it is scraggled and twisted along the coast of Maine.... How in Florida the detours are bright with the sealime of rolled shells.... How the road degrades into a rigorous lattice of country dirt athwart Kansas.... How like a blacksnake in the sun it takes the ridges, the green and dim ravines which are the Cumberlands, and lolls loose in the hot Alabama valleys." Over these roads the restless American people traveled because "We are restive entirely for the sake of restiveness. Whatever we may think, we move for no better reason than for the plain unvarnished hell of it. And there is no better reason." In its analysis *Fortune* also identified a "new objective—motion with the least possible interruption," indicating the impulse for speed and elapsed time that the current interstate highways reflect also existed in the 1930s.

Greyhound responded to two of the most frequent customer complaints about the roadside—the quality of food and the condition of restrooms—creating a network of restaurants and rest stops beginning in 1937. *Bus Transportation*, May 1937, outlined Greyhound's ambitious initial intentions. "Greyhound Bus Lines has organized a new subsidiary called Greyhound Travel Stations, Inc., which is putting into operation a plan to improve and to some degree standardize the 582 rest and lunch stops on their 30,000 mile system." Greyhound intended to issue franchises and then work with managers to update their facilities, "meeting standards of architecture, equipment and service." The article indicated the first remodeled "station" would open at Westport, Connecticut. In addition, Greyhound planned to establish "specially designed" diners at flag stops located approximately every ten miles. Built by J.G. Roy and Sons Company, Springfield, Massachusetts, the intention was to ship pre-fabricated sections for on-site assembly. Unrealistically, Greyhound planned to construct 3,500 diners at the flag stops and have the "entire system" established in five years.

In 1939, Greyhound publicity declared, "Greyhound has created a system of Post Houses—an expanding chain of handsome wayside stops—to provide travelers with food service of high quality at reasonable cost." A folder provided to new employees offered further explanation. "The Greyhound Post Houses is an organization set up to finance owners of lunch and comfort stops along the Greyhound routes. The organization lends money to such owners for the purchase of sufficient and proper equipment for their post houses; so that passengers can be served well-prepared and well-cooked food at minimum cost, and so that sanitary and adequately-equipped rest rooms are available for the use of Greyhound passengers at such stops."

GREYHOUND'S ROADSIDE: THE 1930s

The elements of the 1930s "Great American Roadside" described by *Fortune* prefigured the travel experiences that would undermine notions of the "romance of the road." More significantly, as Americans came to embrace the "new objective" of travel with the "least possible interruption" as a national creed, the possibility for an increasingly prominent role for Greyhound decreased. The interstate highway system, the ubiquitous ownership of the automobile, and the airplane offered the promise of the fulfillment of travel with the "least possible interruption." The bus did not.

The current roadside, located just off the interstate exit and often separate from a town or city, offers many of the same types of goods and services offered to the 1930s traveler. Future fast food fare evident in the offerings to the 1930s traveler noted by *Fortune* included hot dogs, the "Bar-B-Q sandwich," the "hot tamale," the "fried fish sandwich," the ice cream cone, and "frozen sweets stuck to little wooden sticks" that are "chocolate-skinned" or "water-ice" or sherbet. The seeds of the current approach to travel, sown in the 1930s, also included the tourist cabin camp—perhaps named "Mo-Tel"—that prefigured the current Super 8, Holiday Express, or Quality Inn just off the interstate exit.

The Painted Canyon Station in the Bad Lands of western North Dakota. *GBM*

The first Greyhound Post House at Effingham, Illinois. Promoting the Post Houses to stockholders, Greyhound featured this photograph in its 1939 Annual Report. *GBM*

The Greyhound Inn located two miles south of Somerset, Kentucky. *GBM*

The Greyhound Post House located along the four-mile stretch of Highway 15 between Bath and Kanona, New York. *AACA*

The Greyhound Post House that also featured curb service located along New Jersey's western border with Pennsylvania along the Delaware River on Highway 46 near Belvidere, New Jersey, northeast of Bethlehem, Pennsylvania. *AACA*

The Greyhound Wayside Inn at Talbotville, Ontario, Canada. *AACA*

The Greyhound Post House at Westport, Connecticut, near Bridgeport. AACA

CHAPTER 3

1940-1945: THE ROADS OF WAR AND VICTORY

GBM

With an intricate network of routes, Greyhound united the nation physically, culturally, and historically. On the eve of World War II, Greyhound's sponsorship of radio programs utilized another kind of network to promote and encourage travel over this vast network. Various issues of the *Grapevine*, the in-house publication of Pacific Greyhound, publicized "The Romance of the Highways" radio program broadcast Sunday mornings "over 26 stations of the Mutual Don Lee Network." The ongoing references linking travel and "romance" indicate the continued prominence of these notions in Greyhound's marketing efforts.

"Through the Mike...As Well As down the Pike!" announced *Bus Transportation*, March 1940, in its story of another new Greyhound sponsored radio program. The *Grapevine*, offered these highlights. "Greyhound is on the air every Friday evening over the coast-to-coast NBC Blue Network with a brand new radio program just as novel and different as the new Super-Coach itself. It's a natural—from an entertainment standpoint and from Greyhound's standpoint. It is called 'This Amazing America,' which appropriately describes what it's all about. The main feature of the program will be a battle of wits between two teams of typical Americans. Bob Brown, the program's master of ceremonies, gives the clues about historical or geographical interest anywhere in America. Then the contestants in the studio, and the millions of radio listeners all over the nation, try to identify the places from the clues. Successful contestants get cash prizes and radio listeners get a lot of fun. Incidentally there's a way for them to win cash prizes too. The music of Roy Shields and his orchestra and the singing of the Ranch Boys add extra variety and interest to the program."

Greyhound also offered listeners "A new and revised version of the ever-popular folder, 'This Amazing America.'" In addition, "A new, bright, colorful window display featuring the new program will be used in cities where the program is broadcast." Greyhound encouraged its employees to "Get behind 'This Amazing America' with all you've got! It's timely, it's national, it fits Greyhound like a glove. Even it's strictly entertainment features have a travel urge in them [...]. The more that people know about 'This Amazing America,' the more they'll want to

Fig. 125. *GBM*

Fig. 126. *MBS*

see of it, and more people will travel by Greyhound." The context for these efforts was the war in Europe that began on September 1, 1939 with the German invasion of Poland and the subsequent declarations of war against Germany by England and France on September 3rd. The government banned European travel by Americans and President Franklin Delano Roosevelt proclaimed 1940 as "Travel America Year." **[fig. 125]** Greyhound played up the Presidential proclamation, announcing 1940 as "the best year in history for exploring the limitless attractions of your own country." As Americans planned domestic travel and vacations, Greyhound encouraged them with advertisements and information-filled brochures and folders to travel by bus and see "This Amazing America." **[fig. 126]**

The "This Amazing America" folder, initially published in 1938 and updated in 1940, focused on the excitement of visiting the "strange and unusual places reached by Greyhound Lines." The text declared, "America is packed full of strange and exciting places to visit—almost unbelievable curiosities, some man-made, some natural!" The folder reminded poten-

Fig. 127. *MBS*

tial travelers that nothing could compare with seeing the actual places since it offered "just samples of the thrills that make Greyhound travel unique in the sightseeing opportunities it affords." In addition, "When you go anywhere by Greyhound you seem to be in more intimate touch with the scenery and life about you. You get a 'close-up' of America's star attractions—not a take-it-on-the-run glimpse." The folder also promoted the value of thrift. "Believe it or not, Greyhound *shrinks* the map! At least, that's the practical effect of its low fares. You can travel over two miles by Super-Coach at the cost of driving your own car just one mile. That means seeing twice as much for your money. It costs less to 'see America best'—by Greyhound!" The February/March 1940 issue of *The Highway Traveler* featured this colorful advertisement reflecting the "This Amazing America" theme. **[fig. 127]**

Greyhound linked all of its "This Amazing America" travel promotion with the newly introduced "Streamlined Super-Coach...In service on all principal Greyhound routes." The reference to "Streamlined," intended to indicate the traveler could expect to ride in the most modern bus. **[fig. 128]** This 1939 rendering from the "General Motors Styling Section" depicts the new Super-Coach designed to replace the Model 719 and 743 Super-Coaches. Greyhound produced a brochure in 1940 to promote the new bus. "Here's the Newest Greyhound Super-Coach with Perfected Air-Conditioning—the Smooth, Low-Cost Way to See 'This Amazing America.'" Each page featured some rhyming verse. "This coach is out ahead a mile, From front to rear, from roof to aisle, For trips in easy riding style!" This artist's illustration offered potential travelers a look inside the new bus. **[fig. 129]** "America now has a newer, finer way to travel—the recently introduced Super-Coach, new leader of Greyhound's nationwide fleet. It's more than a new bus—it's a new experience in highway travel. It's different—from its sleek streamlined alumilite-finished exterior to its restful, smartly styled, air-conditioned interior—from its retractable step at the front door to the new-type Diesel engine at the rear. The distinctive "alumilite-finished exterior" resulted in eventually identifying the buses by the term "Silversides." **[fig. 130]** Yellow Coach manufactured 37- and 41-passenger versions. Greyhound, covering all the bases, sought to suggest that both the man at the right and the even more attentive woman are paying close attention during an explanation of aspects of the "new-type Diesel"-filled engine bay. **[fig. 131]** The promise of greater fuel economy with diesel engines was of prime importance to Greyhound. In 1940 the Greyhound fleet consumed 40,761,762 gallons of fuel.

Fig. 128. Streamlined Super-Coach. *MBS*

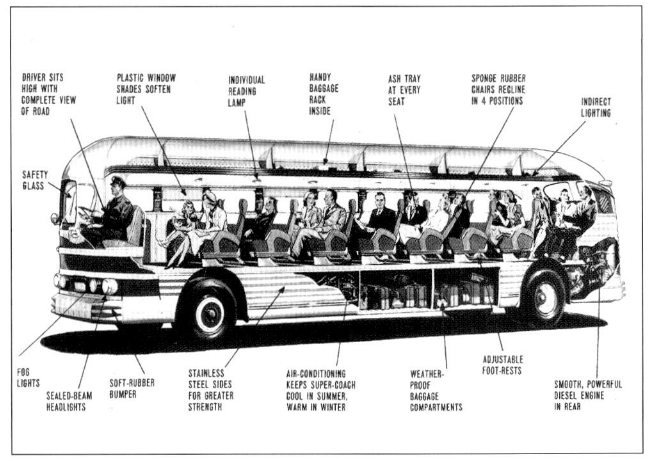

Fig. 129. *GBM*

Fig. 130. 1940 Silversides. *AACA*

Fig. 131. Diesel powered Super-Coach. *GBM*

Fig. 131. This photograph, used in the brochure, illustrated the "spacious comfort" of the new Super-Coach. *AACA*

It would be difficult to underestimate the significance of air-conditioning as an inducement to travel by Greyhound bus. Virtually none of the automobiles on America's roads featured air-conditioning. While simplistic, the second rhyme in the brochure made sense to the potential traveler. "Perfected air-conditioning, Means comfort while you're traveling—In summer, winter, fall or spring! Whatever the weather may be *outside* this luxury liner, it's always a perfect day *inside*." Greyhound explained that the bus featured the "newest-type air-conditioning equipment, thermostatically-controlled." As a result, the system could reduce the inside temperature by up to thirty-five degrees compared to the outside temperature. The brochure also noted "hundreds of Greyhound coaches of other types" featured air-conditioning. Greyhound began equipping the Super-Coaches initially introduced in 1935 with air-conditioning in 1938.

"Your ride in extra comfort's due, To spongy rubber under you—A type of seat that's strictly new!" Features the Greyhound brochure identified included "plenty of room between seats," the individually adjustable five position seats "richly upholstered, in mohair, with new-type sponge rubber cushions," the "12-position foot rest," the "soft and restful indirect lighting" and a "brighter reading light for each passenger." Each seat featured an ashtray indicating passengers could smoke on the bus.

Fig. 132. 1935 Yellow Coach Model 719. *GBM*

Another rhyme, another feature: "Your baggage travels out of sight. It's locked below and weather tight—and makes you feel your traveling light!" The new Silversides Super-Coach continued to feature a "weatherproof baggage compartment" below the passenger deck first introduced on the 1935 Yellow Coach Model 719 Super-Coach. The brochure included the photograph **[fig. 132]** shown as well as a photograph similar to the accompanying photograph illustrating the convenience of passenger loading due to the "retractable step for easy, street-level boarding." Particularly useful for "elderly people and children," the step automatically glided into position as the door opened and retracted as the door closed. **[fig. 133]**

The new Silversides Super-Coach was the means to an end—the opportunity to travel and see "This Amazing America." Greyhound's advertising rhyme declared, "To get the world's most thrilling views, In your own nation, take a cruise, By Super Coach—the bus to choose!" Among the amazing things to see, Greyhound identified the Great Smokies; Florida's Bok Tower; Minnesota's 10,000 lakes; Washington, D.C.; Arizona's Petrified Forest; blind cave-dwelling fish in Mammoth Cave, Kentucky; Old Faithful geyser; Nashville's own Parthenon; the highway from Miami to Key West, Florida; and Michigan's autoless Mackinac Island. Greyhound's 1940 *Annual Report* featured this photograph. **[fig. 134]** While the introductory brochure uses "Super-Coach," the caption indicates a variation in the identification of the new bus: "New Greyhound Supercoach among the Redwoods of California."

Greyhound's promotion of travel as romantic, thrilling, and exciting offered dreams. However, Greyhound also realized that riding in the newest streamlined alumilite-clad Super-Coach with "easy chair" comfort and air-conditioning had to be affordable. To a large extent, Americans in the 1930s and 1940s lim-

Fig. 133. Retractable step for easy, street-level boarding. *GBM*

ited their consumption to purchases they could pay for completely. The ubiquitous credit card in current use did not exist. Today we do not defer the gratification, but instead defer the payment. In the past, travel for pleasure, as with other non-essentials, required the expenditure of carefully marshaled savings. "Your money travels far and wide—It buys a longer Greyhound ride, And gives you extra fun beside!" Greyhound offered this to the potential traveler: "Greyhound fares—far lower than those for any other type of public transportation—are only a fraction of the cost of driving your own car. No wonder Greyhound with its streamlined, air conditioned Super-Coaches is the favorite travel-way of America's vacationists." The result is that "When you spend less going places by Greyhound, you have more money to spend when you get there."

This publicity photograph features a Super-Coach with the New York skyline as a backdrop. In the tableau created to interest potential travelers the "1940 New York World's Fair" logo under the driver's window suggests the final exciting destination—a dream come true. *AACA*

The success of radio's "This Amazing America" resulted in a Technicolor movie of the same name released in 1941. According to Greyhound publicity, the "touromance" was a "knockout!" The 35-minute film, produced by the Hal Roach Studios, Culver City, California, told the story of two contestants of the "This Amazing America" radio show who win free trips by Greyhound to travel "completely around the country." The contestant's travels include Washington, D.C., New York City, Boston, the Natural Bridge in Virginia, the Great Smokies, Lake Itasca in Minnesota, the Alamo, the Grand Canyon, and Hollywood. Greyhound reminded

Fig. 134. Super-Coach among the redwoods of California. *AACA*

its employees that as a "touromance," the film not only "ends where all love stories should, at Niagara Falls," but is a "great value in the promotion of Greyhound travel." Of course, the stars of the movie included the newest Silversides Super-Coach. **[fig. 135]**

This 1941 advertisement introduced the Greyhound team—the agent, the driver, the woman who arranges "everything," and the mechanic—responsible for making "pleasant trips to all this Amazing America!" on a Silversides Super-Coach Greyhound a reality. **[fig. 136]** Also acknowledging the Greyhound team, *The Highway Traveler*, December 1940/ January 1941 offered this advertisement for holiday travel. "Next Stop—*Christmas!* This is the season when each husky Greyhound driver, each busy ticket agent, each overalled mechanic and white-collar clerk gets an extra thrill out of his job! Wouldn't you... doing your share to speed a million people home to happy reunions with family and friends? (Especially when you know you're saving each of them a nice pocketful of change for extra Christmas gifts, extra holiday fun!)" An elderly couple and a mother and

Fig. 135. Silversides Super-Coach, 1941.*GBM*

Fig. 136. *MBS*

Fig. 137. *MBS*

young daughter sit comfortably inside a Super-Coach with an icon-filled winter scene featuring lighted Christmas trees, a church with spire, a school, and mountains outside. **[fig. 137]**

As America moved toward war, Greyhound advertising reflected the changes taking place, increasingly depicting both civilian and military-related travel. This Fall 1941 advertisement declared, "Streamlined Super-Coaches are carrying thousands of workers who are building America's defense—thousands of soldiers, sailors, and marines traveling between their homes and military camps and bases—millions of other Americans in their every-day pursuits." The illustrations reflect the growing concern for national defense, while acknowledging civilian activities. **[fig. 138]**

The theme of national defense became explicit in this advertisement featured in *The Highway Traveler*, June/July 1941. The signs of increased attention to the war in Europe resulted in an advertisement that featured a soldier and a sailor with displays of rank designations. "Greyhound rates TOPS with men in the Service—no matter what their rank or rating! Super-Coach service is the first choice of National defense forces, and workers on defense projects—because Greyhound serves more military camps and bases, more defense areas than any other transportation system. Its low fares fit even a buck private's slender pay—its comfort and efficiency are fit for a general!" The advertisement informed readers about "How YOU Can Aid National Defense: If your personal plans permit, do your vacation or pleasure traveling this summer on WEEKDAYS. You'll be saving extra seat-space for soldiers and sailors on leave—and for National defense workers who can travel best on week-ends." **[fig. 139]** Greyhound also offered folders that featured route maps and the rank designations. **[fig. 140]**

Greyhound's advertising also reflected the nation's preparation for the eventuality of entry into the war. For example, an advertisement in *The Highway Traveler*, August/September 1941 featured an illustration of a soldier on leave just off a Greyhound Super-

GREYHOUND FITS THE
FALL PICTURE OF
America in Action!
EXPRESS
1941
GREYHOUND LINES
The pulse of a nation quickens in the fall . . . especially this nation, and especially this fall!
Never before has the life of America reached such a tremendous tempo. Greyhound is part of this picture, vital to it! Streamlined Super-Coaches are carrying thousands of workers who are building America's defense—thousands of soldiers, sailors, and marines traveling between their homes and military camps and bases —millions of other Americans in their every-day pursuits.
Equally important, motor bus travel conserves material vital to national defense by carrying more people per pound of metal, or of rubber, or of gasoline than is possible by private automobile.
Greyhound does all this at lower fares than for any other kind of transportation—reaching more military areas, cities and communities—than any other travel system.
GREYHOUND
Vital transportation for
National Defense workers
...Service made to measure
for men in the Service!

Fig. 138. *MBS*

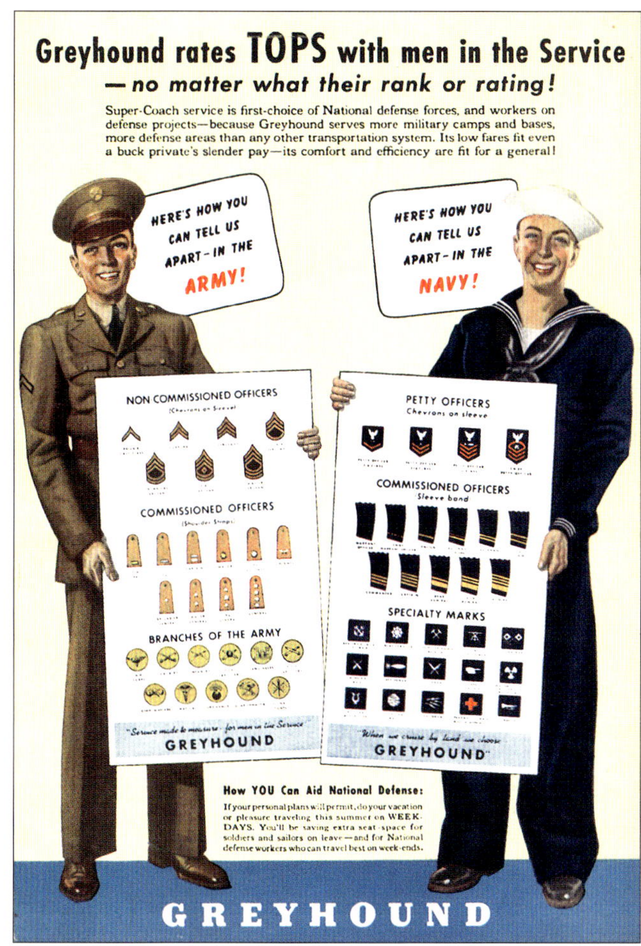

Fig. 139. *MBS*

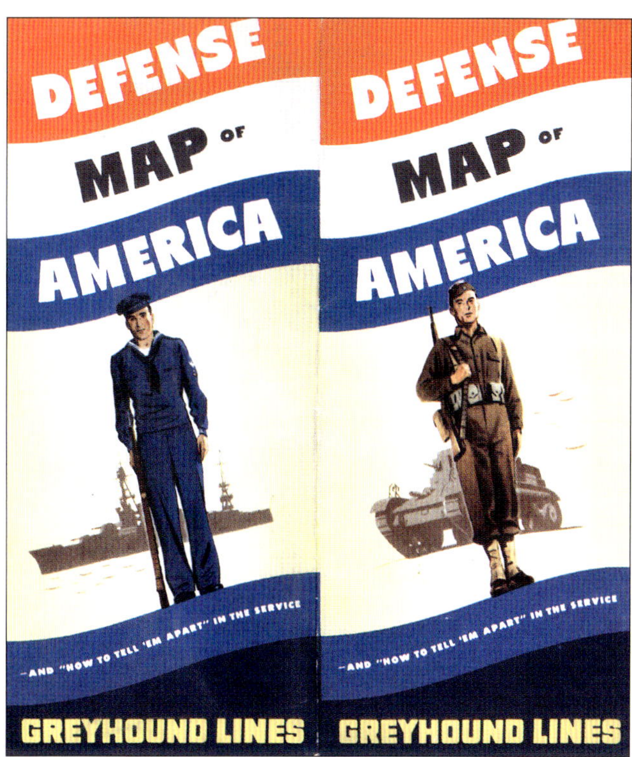

Fig. 140. *MBS*

Coach meeting his parents and best girl. The advertising text elaborated on this tableau indicating the lessons the reader should learn. "SURE ENOUGH! There are mother and dad waiting at the bus door—and it isn't mere chance that brought Anne to the terminal either! Thousands of such heart-warming dramas unfold at Greyhound stations throughout America, as the big Super-Coaches roll in and men in blue or khaki uniforms swarm out eagerly. Frequent time-saving, low-cost visits between men in the Service and their friends and relatives at home mean a tremendous boost to national morale—and that's the first bulwark of defense." "National defense has been decentralized—spread out over all America ...." Finally, "We suggest: if you are visiting your boy at camp, *go Greyhound for comfort, economy, sight-seeing.* If he can get home on furlough, *send him a Greyhound round trip ticket.*"

American entry into World War II for the most part put pleasure travel on hold for "the duration." Greyhound patriotically encouraged the nation to unite in the effort to win the war and allow public transportation to focus on the demands of war. The transportation of large numbers of soldiers and workers essential to the war effort became the challenge for the intercity bus industry in general and Greyhound in particular. The war witnessed a tremendous migration within the United States. Millions relocated to new centers for industrial production to meet the demands of war resulting in dislocation and disruption. In addition, millions of service personnel took leaves, came home to visit their families, and returned to military installations. While transporting military personnel limited civilian travel, other factors also influenced wartime bus use. Rationing of gasoline, tires, and various metals and materials impacted not just Greyhound, but the entire motor vehicle and transportation industry. Manpower shortages—key personnel were now in the military—also proved significant.

Following America's entry into the war, the National Association of Motor Bus Operators (NAMBO) published *Intercity Buses at War.* Designed to put the best face on the efforts of the intercity bus industry in wartime, the book offers a unique view of the culture of the nation at war. The report offers the story of the intercity bus industry and Americans patriotically responding to the challenges of war—joined together in a common cause to win the war.

On the home front, *Intercity Buses at War* noted how bus companies successfully adapted to the profound changes brought on by the war. "During the first few months of hostilities, production facilities grew on a scale never before approached. Out along the highways, in all parts of the country, new plants sprang up to make explosives, tanks, shells, airplanes and guns. Existing factories rapidly converted from peacetime products to materials of war. Old shipyards were enlarged and new ones built. In all these activities, buses played a major part. They carried construction crews to their jobs of building or converting the factories that would help America deliver 'enough on time.' As rapidly as great new war plants were completed, buses brought manpower to begin their production and keep them running." In addition, the war resulted in the decentralization of defense plants throughout the United States. "Almost over-night new industries have appeared, far from the usual sources of manpower. New housing projects have been completed, new cities have been born. And it is to the bus lines that these industries and communities look for essential public passenger service."

While carried out on the home front, the bus industry's support for the war front proved significant. "At the same time, buses also were helping to build the greatest U.S. fighting force in history [...]. [B]uses were assigned the task of moving the great majority of selectees from home towns to induction centers." Crucial to building and maintaining morale, buses also carried military personnel on leaves and furloughs as well as relatives to camps for visits. Rationing significantly impacted the use of privately owned automobiles resulting in the greater use of buses and rail passenger service. The report noted, "In normal times, about eighty-five percent of all people traveling from one city to another did so by private automobile." However, in 1942, buses transported 692,000,000 passengers, compared to 396,000,000 passengers for the largest peacetime year.

While extolling the value of cooperation the report raised questions about the impact of some wartime measures. In December 1942, a national maximum speed limit of 35 miles per hour was established. Designed to save fuel and conserve rubber, the limit did achieve savings for private automobiles. Significantly for the National Association of Motor Bus Operators, this was not the case for intercity buses. Specifically, "*no appreciable savings in rubber or fuel have been realized.* This is due to the fact that buses are radically different from private automobiles in both design and operation." While automobiles can run in high gear at speeds below 35 miles per hour, buses cannot. At these lower speeds more gear shifting is required, resulting in greater wear on tires, transmissions, engines, and brakes. The report noted tests conducted by "one of the large bus companies" verified these claims. In fact, Greyhound conducted these tests. "Each bus now must spend about thirty percent more time completing a trip of any given distance. This means a marked decrease in the number of trips a bus can make, and a corresponding decrease in the number of passengers a bus can transport in any given period." In a monumental undertaking, the system-wide schedules of the intercity bus lines all required adjustment.

Intercity Buses at War drew attention to the limited number of intercity buses manufactured despite the increased passenger volume. The report noted that in the five years prior to Pearl Harbor yearly average production totaled 2,277 buses. In 1942, the industry produced 3,968 intercity buses, but in 1943, production totaled zero. The War Production Board authorized approximately 1,825 intercity buses for 1944. This lack of production of new buses resulted in the return to service of "retired" buses. These older buses required excessive maintenance and resources compared to newer buses.

Fortune's September 1944 article, "Greyhound: Still Growing" is a look through the lens of war. "The intercity bus business, unlike the railroad passenger business, has been on the ascendant for two decades. War made the railroad passenger train profitable for the first time in years, but it only accelerated the climb of the bus business to new levels of volume and profit. Unlike most railroad men, busmen are dead sure they will keep climbing after the war. And no company is more optimistic, and with more reason, than the colossus of the industry, known perhaps less derisively than respectfully as "the Hound." When *Fortune* first covered Greyhound in 1934, "it was chasing after 15 percent of the intercity bus business and breathing hard. Today it is running more than 35 percent of the business, which itself has grown by leaps and bounds. Greyhound's 4,000 buses, each painted the familiar blue and white and wearing the dashing hound on its side, call regularly at terminals in more than 6,000 cities, towns, and villages with a combined population nearly half that of the U.S.. Their 64,700 miles of routes, nearly five times greater than any U.S. railroad and more than a fourth of the entire U.S. railroad mileage, give them a national coverage far more comprehensive than any other transportation enterprise in our history."

Fortune also noted that in World War I, the intercity bus industry did not exist and railroads "hauled all intercity passengers." In World War II, *Fortune* observed, "there are more intercity busses on U.S. highways than passenger coaches on the rails. These busses call at many more U.S. communities than all the railroads combined. They hauled millions of rural selectees to induction centers, serviced training camps and Army and Navy bases where no railroads ran. They transported millions of war workers to huge new factories that necessarily had to be built at distances from metropolitan railroad passenger terminals; and when the plants were far from housing, the busmen set up regular daily commuting schedules. A good deal of their wartime traffic consisted of carrying visitors to distantly stationed servicemen and war workers." In what seems to contradict current notions, *Fortune* observed, "the biggest single factor in their boom is doubtless wartime prosperity. Millions of people with no urgent objective have been able to afford bus trips, and, despite official warnings, are making the most of their opportunities." This advertisement reflects the issues developed in the *Fortune* article. **[fig. 141]**

Greyhound contended with situations unique to wartime, including a lack of new buses and few new parts. Greyhound also struggled with servicing and repair problems. According to *Fortune*, Greyhound planned to establish reclamation and rebuilding plants all over the country, but couldn't get machinery. Only one plant, set up in Chicago late in 1943, accepted the broken or worn-out parts from every one of the 105 Greyhound garages. In its 1942 *Annual Report* Greyhound explained the process of "metalizing." This involved "spraying molten metal on the roughened surface of the worn part until the required dimensions have been restored. It is then machined to proper size." This process allowed Greyhound to recycle used parts such as pistons, crankshafts, water pump shafts, and transmission shafts previously discarded, and re-machining them to their original size.

Like others, Greyhound lost men to the armed services and employment in war plants including a large proportion of its 6,000 experienced drivers and hundreds of maintenance men. In all, over 5,000 Greyhound personnel served in the military. The 1942 *Annual Report* dealt with Greyhound's response. "The Greyhound companies last year began the employment of women in many occupations which heretofore have been filled only by men. Women are now being employed as drivers in local bus service in California, and at locations throughout the country as collectors on buses serving war plants, in stockrooms, as drivers of service cars, for changing oil and cleaning buses, as hostlers in garages, and as ticket sellers, and the like. No women are as yet being used as drivers on long inter-city routes."

As might be expected, expenses increased. The price of gas, oil, tires, and labor were higher. "In 1940 it cost 22 cents, including depreciation, to operate a bus a mile. [In 1944] it costs 28 cents, or about 30 percent more."

As bus service became part of the larger effort to end "Axis aggression," Greyhound advertising reflected this priority. Greyhound "signed up for the duration." Its advertisements reflected wartime priorities—war needs came first. Following the Japanese attack on Pearl Harbor, December 7, 1941, the U.S. entered World War II. Specifically, Greyhound explained the change in advertising in the 1942 *Annual Report.*

Throughout 1942 Greyhound advertising has sharply changed in its nature and objective. On December 7, 1941, all advertising plans promoting scenic and pleasure travel were dropped, and Greyhound embarked at once on a campaign to:

1. *Pledge Greyhound's whole-hearted cooperation in the war effort and explain the important part buses must take in any successful plan to move manpower in the volume required by war conditions.*
2. *Educate the public to mid-week travel, proper selection of schedules, and the avoidance of holiday and peak-season trips.*
3. *Point out the basic economy of bus travel, especially in its use of such critical materials as rubber, fuel and metals.*
4. *Maintain the strength and prestige of the Greyhound name against the time when competitive conditions will return.*

THE SATURDAY EVENING POST

This ARMY MOVES BY GREYHOUND

. . . 132 Million Passengers in One Year . . . the Fighting, Working Manpower of America!

It will amaze many to learn that Greyhound and the other bus lines now carry more than half of all ***intercity*** passengers moved by public transportation in the United States . . . between cities, towns, military centers, farm and factory areas. Buses do this immensely important job on less than 3 percent of the motor fuel used by all commercial vehicles!

This means that America's great highways have come to the rescue of wartime transportation, enabling it to accomplish its toughest task of all history ***without a serious breakdown.***

Greyhound, doing the largest single share of this war job (132 million passengers last year), has seen its bus riders change, almost overnight, to war plant workers, men and women in uniform, farm help—and all the others whose trips are so necessary to back our fighting men in far lands.

But Greyhound and all bus lines are faced by serious curtailments of equipment and fuel—by loss of skilled personnel—by the national reduction in operating speeds. These restrictions have cut deeply into motor buses' capacity for carrying manpower.

The Office of Defense Transportation and the intercity bus lines, working together, are doing all they can to remedy this threat to the war program. ***But you, the man or woman who reads this, can help most of all:*** by avoiding all travel around holidays—by taking necessary trips on midweek days (Tuesday, Wednesday, Thursday)—by traveling light—by accepting occasional inconvenience or crowding with good nature.

And buy more War Savings Bonds! They're the best investment for you, for your country—and they'll be good for thrilling travel in the finer, faster Greyhound buses Victory will bring.

GREYHOUND

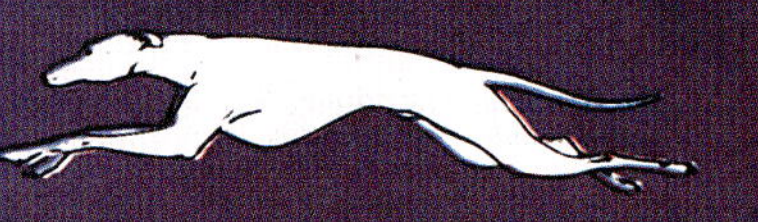

Fig. 141. *GBM*

Fig. 142. *Author's Collection*

Fig. 143. *GBM*

The new advertising approach began to appear in early 1942. In this advertisement from that period, Greyhound promoted its role "IN ACTIVE SERVICE for America's Two Great Armies! *There's a big job to be done*—and today Greyhound Super-Coach travel lends itself wholeheartedly to the needs of America's military and civilian armies." "*To the men in the fighting forces*—Greyhound's frequent, low-cost, nation-wide service means a saving of precious time, and money, too, when furloughs at home are granted. *To the millions in the civilian army*—travel by motor coach has become a vital necessity. By bus, war workers travel to jobs, farmers to markets, students to school. On business or for much-needed recreation, still others reach thousands of communities served by no other type of public transportation." **[fig. 142]**

"See America Now!" became "Serve America Now!" The female Greyhound worker, wearing a "V" for victory pin, has altered the slogan to reflect the realities of wartime. By Serving America now "you can see America later" and invest the money saved in U.S. War Bonds or Stamps. The increased passenger loads that reflected the demands of war meant Greyhound could not accommodate any significant levels of civilian pleasure travel. Advertisements sought to remind Americans of the priorities necessitated by war. "Think twice before you do any unnecessary traveling. Take trips *before* or *after* the mid-summer rush period if possible...travel on Monday, Tuesday, Wednesday, or Thursday, leaving the week-end for war workers and men in uniform." "The people Greyhound is carrying *and intends to carry efficiently* are selectees, fighting men, war workers, essential business travelers—all those who must keep rolling *to keep America rolling!*" In case the reader missed the point, the 1942 advertisement declared, "The war effort comes first with Greyhound." **[fig. 143]**

Greyhound advertising sought to inform the public about the changing circumstances due to the increasing travel by military personnel and civilian war workers. Reminding readers that there are appropriate times to travel if you are planning "purely sightseeing trips in time of war," this 1942 advertisement declared, "You do Two Good Turns when you travel on mid-week days...1—for the war workers and men in uniform who often can travel only on weekends" and "2—for yourself... avoiding inconvenience, delay and crowded buses." In the advertising tableau the Marine in uni-

Fig. 144. *MBS*

Fig. 145. *GBM*

form indicates it is a weekend. The woman is thus a traveling war worker since Greyhound promoted pleasure travel on mid-week days. **[fig. 144]** Reflecting these same themes and offering an all-too-common tableau, this advertisement features a meeting of a mother and son who will soon part. Greyhound travelers could do their part to help America by making such visits possible. **[fig. 145]**

Constructed during World War II, the Alaska-Canadian (Alcan) Highway linked the United States with the Alaska Territory through Canada. Significant strategic value existed because of the location of Alaska in relationship to northern Japan. Major fighting between the United States and Japan occurred in the Aleutian Islands, the island chain that extends southwest of the Alaskan mainland. The government authorized construction of the Alcan Highway in February 1942. The U.S. Army Corps of Engineers, civilian workers of the Public Roads Administration, and private contractors completed the basic construction of the 1,600-plus mile highway from Dawson Creek, British Columbia, to Fairbanks, Alaska, by November 1942. Work continued through the fall of 1943 to make it an all-weather road. Greyhound sought to inform the public that its "familiar blue-and-white buses are rolling on that highway—doing an important job for Uncle Sam, along the most amazing military road of all history." Reflecting prevailing wartime attitudes, the advertisement declared the Alcan Highway is "America's pledge to the world that we'll run the greedy little Japs clear back to Tokyo and beyond." It also expressed Greyhound's optimism about the postwar world: "After Victory comes, who can doubt that roads and buses will work together to develop the wonderland of Western Canada and Alaska." **[fig. 146]**

In 1943 this image would resonate with millions. A young woman—someone's sister or wife—at the rural mailbox with at least one V-Mail letter clutched in her hand—a connection with one or more of the three service personnel represented by the three blue stars on the placard attached to the mailbox post. The long line of military vehicles on the highway, a reminder that the nation was at war—the result of a "sneak attack"—and the Silversides Super-Coach evidence of

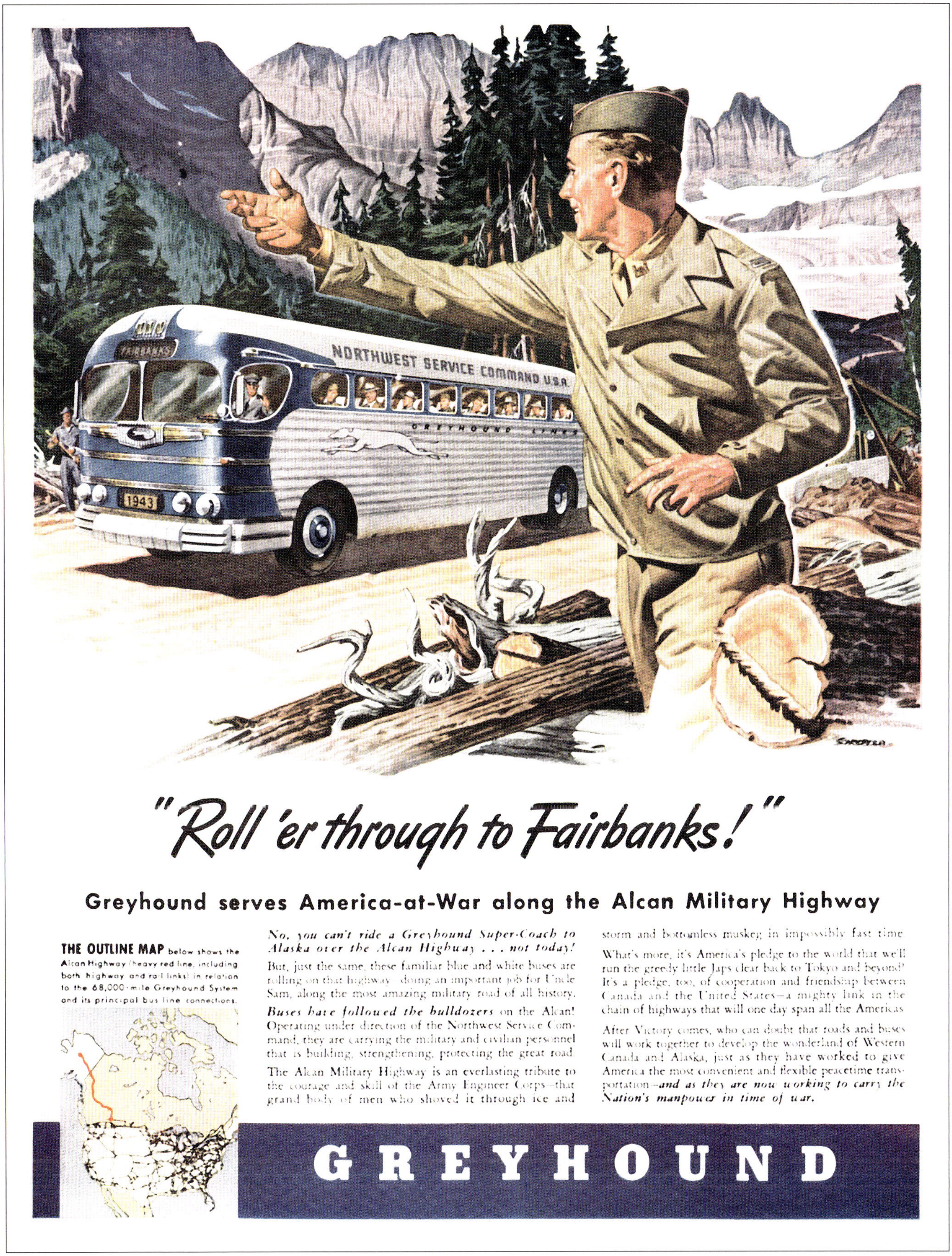

"Roll 'er through to Fairbanks!"

Greyhound serves America-at-War along the Alcan Military Highway

THE OUTLINE MAP below shows the Alcan Highway (heavy red line, including both highway and rail links) in relation to the 68,000-mile Greyhound System and its principal bus line connections.

No, you can't ride a Greyhound Super-Coach to Alaska over the Alcan Highway . . . not today!

But, just the same, these familiar blue-and-white buses are rolling on that highway—doing an important job for Uncle Sam, along the most amazing military road of all history.

Buses have followed the bulldozers on the Alcan! Operating under direction of the Northwest Service Command, they are carrying the military and civilian personnel that is building, strengthening, protecting the great road.

The Alcan Military Highway is an everlasting tribute to the courage and skill of the Army Engineer Corps—that grand body of men who shoved it through ice and storm and bottomless muskeg in impossibly fast time.

What's more, it's America's pledge to the world that we'll run the greedy little Japs clear back to Tokyo and beyond! It's a pledge, too, of cooperation and friendship between Canada and the United States—a mighty link in the chain of highways that will one day span all the Americas.

After Victory comes, who can doubt that roads and buses will work together to develop the wonderland of Western Canada and Alaska, just as they have worked to give America the most convenient and flexible peacetime transportation—***and as they are now working to carry the Nation's manpower in time of war.***

GREYHOUND

Fig. 146. *Author's Collection*

Fig. 147. *GBM*

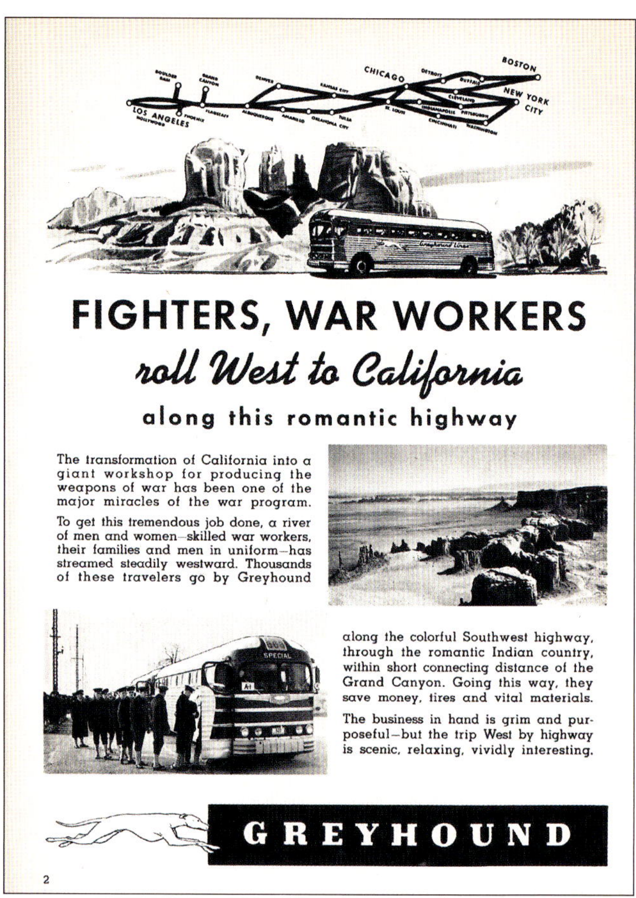

Fig. 148. *MBS*

the important role played by Greyhound in the war effort. The advertisement reflects the wartime goals established by Greyhound in 1942. "Greyhound's whole-hearted cooperation in the war effort," touted that it and "other bus lines carried three-quarters of a billion passengers last year" and "most of them were selectees, men in uniform, war workers, farmers, nurses…whose trips…were essential to the war effort." Explaining Greyhound's contribution helped to "Maintain the strength and prestige of the Greyhound name against the time when competitive conditions will return." The advertisement also offered an assurance that it was ready for the challenges of a competitive postwar era: "And you can look to Greyhound for a brand new chapter in scenic, convenient, economical travel—*after Victory is won.*" **[fig. 147]** The advertisement also features a small reproduction of an advertisement from the 1930s promoting travel to see "This Amazing America." (**See page 77.**) America is still amazing because of the "grim will of its people to win this war." Greyhound offers a new credo for America: "SERVE America now—so you can SEE America later!"

The theme of "the romance of the road," offered as a counterpoint to dislocation and disruption, continued during the war. The massive migration of men and women to work or train as members of the military became an opportunity for "going the Greyhound way" and to "roll West to California along this romantic highway." These travelers could "go by Greyhound along the colorful Southwest highway, through the romantic Indian country." Of course the "business in hand is grim and purposeful—but the trip West by highway is scenic, relaxing, vividly interesting." **[fig. 148]**

Proud of its contributions to the war effort, Greyhound used this advertisement to feature a driver, one of its 5,180 employees serving as "good soldiers, sailors, marines and flyers." The promise of a wonderful postwar future awaits this soldier as well as the traveling public. "My old dispatcher at Greyhound writes me that they're planning the finest passenger buses the U.S.A. has ever seen—and he says they'll want me back there to pilot one of 'em." **[fig. 149]**

This early 1944 advertisement depicted a tableau of wartime unity and harmony, something overly optimistic wartime propaganda suggested would continue with

"I drove a Greyhound
..I'll drive one again!"
"Before I started driving this tank-buster for Uncle Sam, I was what they call a *'Ten-Year Man'* with the Greyhound system. That means ten solid years behind the wheel of those big blue-and-white buses—without once nicking a fender or scraping the paint. The fine points of skill and safety I learned on that job have helped me pull this tank destroyer (and some of my buddies) through a lot of tight scrapes in North Africa and Normandy.
"My old dispatcher at Greyhound writes me that they're planning the finest passenger buses the U. S. A. has ever seen—and he says they'll want me back there to pilot one of 'em. *So watch for me at the wheel when you go traveling, after Victory!*"
The special skills of more than 5,000 Greyhound employees have helped make them good soldiers, sailors, marines and flyers. Greyhound is going to be proud to have these men and women back, in the better days ahead!
5180
GREYHOUND

Fig. 149. *MBS*

A Ski Trooper in Alaska, a Russian officer in Moscow, a lovely senorita in South America, a shirtless Marine somewhere in the Pacific—these are typical of the millions who are today seeing Greyhound's color film "This Amazing America." An Army Chaplain in Alaska writes: "I have shown it at outposts . . . in hospitals . . . on transports . . . before battles. The men have always enthused . . . Thank you for this contribution to morale."

They're still seeing THIS AMAZING AMERICA *All Over the World!*

WHAM! Pearl Harbor stopped sightseeing and pleasure travel all over this land—turned the energies and facilities of the Greyhound Bus System into the urgent job of carrying war-manpower. But that didn't stop Americans—especially the millions in uniform—from dreaming about the magnificent land for which they are fighting. It didn't stop allied and neighboring nations from wanting more intimate information about the fabulous and fascinating U. S. A. Greyhound's Technicolor film "This Amazing America" has helped satisfy that hunger for nearly 11 million people—many thousands of them in the armed forces at home and on scattered battle fronts—more than a million of them in friendly South America (through the efforts of the Coordinator of Inter-American Affairs)—others in such strategic places as the U. S. Embassy at Moscow.

Yet such pictures, however beautiful, are only a stop-gap for the travel-starved millions who will, after victory, revel in the scenic loveliness of this continent. *When that great day comes, look to Greyhound for pleasant, sightseeing travel by highway to all America—at a new high level of luxury and convenience.*

NOTE: Many schools, clubs, churches (having 16mm sound projectors) are anxious to borrow the film "This Amazing America." But prints are hard to obtain—and the armed forces come first. If you like, direct your request to Greyhound Information Center, 1505 N.B.C. Building, Cleveland, Ohio—we'll do our best to fill it.

GREYHOUND

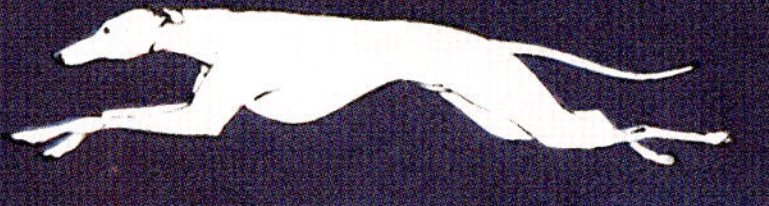

Fig. 150. *GBM*

Fig. 151. *Author's Collection*

Fig. 152. *MBS*

peace. A shirtless Marine, a Russian Officer, and a parka-clad Ski Trooper—along with a "lovely senorita in South America," watch a film. "They're still seeing THIS AMAZING AMERICA *All Over the World!*" Released in 1941 the film told the story of two contestants of the "This Amazing America" radio show who win free trips by Greyhound. As the advertisement notes, "Pearl Harbor stopped sightseeing travel all over this land—turned the energies and facilities of the Greyhound Bus System into the urgent job of carrying war-manpower." This reflects Greyhound's 1942 pledge of "whole-hearted cooperation in the war effort." The advertisement also discusses the dreams of a wonderful postwar future and the desirability of America as a model for the rest of the world. "But that didn't stop millions of American's from dreaming about the magnificent land for which they were fighting. It didn't stop allied and neighboring nations from wanting more intimate information about the fabulous and fascinating U.S.A. Greyhound's Technicolor film 'This Amazing America,' has helped satisfy that hunger for nearly 11 million people." Greyhound supplied the film to the military first, and recognized that the film was only a "stop-gap for the travel-starved millions who will, after victory, revel in the scenic loveliness of this continent. *When that great day comes, look to Greyhound....*" This final point reflects Greyhound's wartime objective of maintaining "the strength and prestige of the Greyhound name." **[fig. 150]**

In military nomenclature "prime movers" denoted transportation equipment crucial to the war effort. As this 1944 advertisement illustrates, Greyhound included the Silversides Super-Coach in this elite company. "On the critical home front Greyhound buses are just as truly prime movers of fighting Americans, whether these men and women are in uniform, in working slacks and jumpers, or in plain business suits." **[fig. 151]**

Nearly two and a half years into the war, the possibility of an end to the war and an Allied victory seemed more likely. This 1944 Greyhound advertisement compared the job of a member of the armed forces and the similar activity he could enjoy in the wonderful peacetime to follow. **[fig. 152]** The "human semaphore who swings a pair of flags on a carrier's deck is guiding home fighting planes in the

WORTH FIGHTING FOR!

The way you plan travel today can hasten his return to scenes he loves

"What are you fighting for, Private Jones?"

"I'm fighting for the ones I love—for my country—for the way I want to live... and that includes a slew of things I haven't time to talk about right now, Mister!"

But you can bet that among the rewards of his coming Victory are the outdoor sports, the scenic thrills to be found in the splendor of America's national parks and playgrounds, scattered all the way from the Maine Coast to the High Sierras. Ten to one, Private Jones already has a spot picked out in the timbered back country, where the trout flash in the shallows, where the air is like wine—a hideout reached only by highway (chosen for a honeymoon, maybe)—and served by the finer, more luxurious Greyhound buses Private Jones can expect after the war's over.

In addition to the many things you are already doing to speed his return to the people and the life he loves, here's one more: ***You can help transportation do its immense war-time job at top efficiency.***

First, you can avoid unnecessary trips—***especially in the crowded mid-summer season.*** If you're taking a needed "civilian furlough", skip July and August if possible. Start and finish any trip on mid-week days (Tuesday, Wednesday, Thursday). Take as little baggage as possible. Get trip information several days in advance. ***And how about planning your vacation on a farm, at Harvest time? You'll be helping America feed its fighting men!***

GREYHOUND

Fig. 153. *GBM*

Fig. 154. *GBM*

Fig. 155. *GBM*

far Pacific. *He's speeding the day* when he can again swing a tennis racket, or a golf club, or a casting rod at some sunny Southern resort in the good old U.S.A.!" In case you missed the point, the advertisement notes, "He and his buddies all over the globe are *speeding that day* the hard and dangerous way." The advertisement reminds the reader of the real cost of the war and the obligation that entails. "Nothing we can do or say can repay their sacrifices… but each of us who tackles his war job at home with all his strength (and keeps buying War Bonds) is helping them bring Victory nearer." And finally, the optimistic belief in the final outcome: "And when victory comes, Greyhound will help to bring 'em home—to their very doorsteps in big cities, small towns and farms all over the land."

Following a similar format, these advertisements illustrate the wonderful peacetime world those who were risking their lives could expect when they came home. **[fig. 153]** Some of the cultural references in these advertisements are no longer part of our cultural ethos. The phrase, "*ask the man who downs one,*" derives from the advertising slogan used by Packard, one of America's premiere luxury cars in the 1940s—"Ask the man who owns one." **[fig. 154]**

A popular wartime song expressed hope for a peaceful post war future: "When the lights go on again all over the world." Greyhound's advertisement at Christmastime 1944, six months after D-Day, reflected this hope. While Americans had more reason to hope that victory would come in 1945, it was still a Christmas of separation from loved ones. Service flags with blue stars hung in the windows of millions of homes. Greyhound offered this poignant tableau of hopeful anticipation of the "greatest home-coming of all time." The "little-boy-at-the-window" and his mother offer this pledge: "*We'll keep it shining… until our soldier comes home!*" The various lights—the candle, the headlights of the Greyhound—are all symbols of the "Millions of other lights [that] are coming on again all over this battered planet." According to the advertisement, these lights also "reflect the hope that shines in the eyes of people everywhere." When victory comes, Greyhound will help bring "our victorious fighters" home. **[fig. 155]**

THE HIGHWAY TRAVELER

In addition to the advertisements inside, the covers of Greyhound's *The Highway Traveler* magazine reflected its pledge of "whole-hearted cooperation in the war effort." The magazine, intended to encourage travel via Greyhound, featured pilots **[fig. 156]**, sailors **[fig. 157]**, and a color-enhanced version of the iconic Joe Rosenthal photograph of the flag raising on Iwo Jima. **[fig. 158]** The June/July 1942 cover is of particular interest**. [fig. 159]** It featured the American flag prominently on display with the United States Supreme Court building in the background. This cover was part of a larger effort to promote patriotism. In response to the Japanese attack on Pearl Harbor and America's subsequent entry into war, approximately three hundred magazines took part in the "United We Stand" campaign, agreeing to feature the American flag on their covers for the July 1942 issue. Paul MacNamara, publicist for Hearst magazines promoted the idea, which gained support from the National Publishers Association, the United States Flag Association, and even the Secretary of the Treasury, Henry Morgenthau, who also encouraged magazines to promote the sale of war bonds and savings stamps to help fund the war.

Fig. 156. *MBS*

Fig. 157. *MBS*

Fig. 158. *MBS*

Fig. 159. *MBS*

All images courtesy Motor Bus Society

This October 1945 cover celebrates the end of the war. The public can now "Travel Victory highways." A Silver-sides Super-Coach moves off toward the distant horizon on a four-lane divided highway, the romantic road to travel into a glorious postwar future. *MBS*

GREYHOUND'S ROADSIDE: 1940-1945

This 1940 photograph features the reported first rest stop established by Greyhound, located in Springfield, Massachusetts. The Model 743 Super-Coach displays the 1940 World's Fair logo, also featured on the buses designed specifically for the Fair. *AACA*

Traveling along U.S. Highway 36 in 1941 Greyhound passengers could stop at this Post House in Newcomerstown, Ohio. *AACA*

The Greyhound passengers traveling to Alpena, Michigan, on Lake Huron have stopped at the Post House Restaurant in Standish, Michigan, in the 1940s. *AACA*

Mackinaw City, Michigan, at the northernmost tip of Lower Michigan where Lake Michigan and Lake Huron meet, featured this Greyhound Post House for travelers going to or from Michigan's Upper Peninsula. *GBM*

1943
postcard sent from
Mackinaw City, Michigan. *GBM*

Greyhound Terminal Album: 1940-1945

Impacted by World War II, Greyhound continued planned terminal construction only through 1942. Terminal design continued to reflect modernism and aspects of the aesthetic of "Streamline Moderne" as defined by Frank E. Wrenick in his analysis of Architect William Sudwick Arrasmith. The terminals built during this period, while still retaining the distinctive "Greyhound look," usually featured limestone facing and angular corners replacing blue porcelain panels and rounded corners.

The opening of a new terminal provided an opportunity for Greyhound to showcase the amenities and ambiance associated with bus travel. *Bus Transportation*, November 1940, covered one such event in "A Georgia Peach...Atlanta's New Terminal." The article reported that more than 35,000 people visited the Atlanta Greyhound Terminal on its formal opening day. In fact, "it was necessary to call out extra police in order to handle the crowds." Greyhound rewarded the visitors with "roses to the ladies, balloons to the children, and key rings to the men," all distributed by "six hostesses in blue and white capes and overseas caps." In addition, "one of the newest RCA radios, a small-type battery portable known as the 'Personal Model,' was given away each hour from 1 o'clock until 10 o'clock, with six being given away during the height of the crowd at 8. Registration tickets with coupons bore duplicate numbers, and each visitor was asked to fill one out with his name and address, detaching the stub for identification. The huge box in which the coupons were placed was closed five minutes before the hour, shaken up in front of the audience, and a ticket was drawn by some child selected from the audience." You had to be present to win and the coupons were good for each drawing. As a result, "many stayed throughout the day in an effort to win one of the radios." A "Hammond Electric Organ and one of Atlanta's outstanding organists" provided music.

According to *Bus Transportation*, the $300,000 terminal, designed by Wischmeyer, Arrasmith & Elswick of Louisville, and located "in the very heart of Atlanta's business district, is said to be one of the most modern in the country. Modernistic in design, it is constructed of lightfaced brick, chrome aluminum, glass brick and a composition similar to Bakelite. The terminal is fully air conditioned throughout." The general public's interest in the opening of a bus terminal is indicative of the recognition that the terminal was a part of the adventure of travel.

Like similar facilities located throughout the South, the terminal, following long established custom and practice, accommodated "Jim Crow." *Bus Transportation* noted the basement featured segregated facilities including "shower rooms in addition to colored rest rooms. A colored waiting room and restaurant are situated on one side of the terminal."

Washington, D.C. *GBM*

Baltimore, Maryland. *GBM*

AACA

Syracuse, New York. *AACA*

GBM

CHAPTER 4

1945-1954: The Roads to Peace and Prosperity

MBS

Peace! Soldiers and sailors imagined coming home to fulfill their idea of the American dream—a wife and family, a well-paying job, a new house and possibly a college education with the assistance of the 1944 GI Bill—all part of their well-earned share of the cornucopia of consumer goods available after the return to civilian production.

The Great Depression and World War II had created nearly fifteen years of economic abnormality. The Great Depression resulted in severe economic hardship for millions. Additional millions, while still employed, found financial resources limited. Goods remained on store shelves. The demands of World War II for a work force—as soldiers or war industry workers—created full employment. Incomes increased, but rationing of various products and materials limited the supply of civilian goods—the needs of the war came first. In some respects the abnormalities continued into the postwar. Millions of soldiers returned home. The elimination of wartime regulations and restrictions and the transition to the peacetime production of consumer goods resulted in disruption and dislocation, just as the war had done. Inflation proved a particularly troublesome problem. However, while some worried about a postwar depression replicating the initial period following World War I, most Americans optimistically looked forward to peace and prosperity.

Greyhound celebrated the end of the war; its advertisements mirrored the joy felt by millions. "I'll be home for Christmas!" The portion of this song's lyrics, that said, "If only in my dreams," had reflected the realities of war. Now the portion, "You can count on me," had come true. This Greyhound advertising tableau depicts the dream of millions. "Crowd in closer little fellow—your daddy's home! This is the brightest Christmas in your lifetime—with the black shadow of war lifted from all our hearts, millions of our men rolling home [...]." The candle burning in the window, now a symbol of a long held hope for peace on earth, meant *he* was home. Greyhound, of course, helped "speed the reunions of fighting men with their loved ones." While it was the time to celebrate victory, Greyhound, like the returning GIs, looked to a future bright with promise. "From here on in, we invite you to watch for further bus improvements and innovations. *They're coming fast, and Greyhound will lead the way.*" **[fig. 160]**

With peace the soldier could say, "I fought for this... one day I'm going to see and enjoy all of it!"

Fig. 160. *GBM*

Fig. 161. *GBM*

The "nightmare of battle" made the dreams of a glorious future possible. Having offered their lives for their country, America's "returning fighters" contributed to a "rebirth of pride and interest in our homeland." Hopefully, seeing the USA meant traveling by Greyhound—the only question to consider, "Will travelers ride in the Silversides Super-Coach shown in the advertisement or in 'Motor coaches of startling new design, now taking definite shape?'" The actual production of new postwar buses would represent the tangible evidence that dreams could come true. **[fig. 161]**

The war resulted in an outpouring of creative dreams about the postwar future for American business. During the war, advertisements by many businesses promised both full devotion to the war effort and, with peace and the return to civilian production, a new and better future. In keeping with the general desire to offer a positive response to the difficulties of wartime, *Intercity Buses at War,* published late in the war by the National Association of Motor Bus Operators (NAMBO), offered its optimistic vision of a brighter day ahead: "After Victory—A New Day of Travel. America will win this war. The days of carefree, peacetime travel will come again. Those days will bring new comfort and convenience in bus travel, and a host of new scenic wonders to explore on the highways."

Without acknowledging Greyhound, the report noted innovations actually under development by Greyhound. "New streamlined and air-conditioned buses for post-war service are already taking form on designer's drawing boards, and in the mind's of engineers." In addition, "Helicopter 'Air Buses' may even supplement the highway routes and bring air transportation to millions of people in thousands of towns and cities. Such service could be developed as 'feeders' to the global air lines of tomorrow so that the far corners of the world will be measured only in hours."

Reflecting utopian visions similar to the General Motors' Futurama exhibit at the New York World's Fair on the eve of World War II, as well as the reality of the Alcan Highway, the report also envisioned a network of new highways. "Even so, the highways will still continue to be the right-of-way for the American traveler. Up through Alaska and down through neighbor nations to the south, new high-

Fig. 162. *GBM*

ways will sometime soon, invite every American to sample the pleasures of international highway travel. When that time comes, the present difficulties and inconveniences of wartime travel will be forgotten."

The NAMBO report also noted, "Plans are being made for spacious new terminals and garages throughout the country—a program of expansion that will provide post-war employment for thousands. With these new facilities, an hour's trip to a nearby city or a transcontinental sightseeing tour will offer added pleasures in travel."

Another trade organization, the Motor Bus Lines of America, offered its own conception of the bus and travel in the postwar future, "Over Highways of Tomorrow." **[fig. 162]**

Utopian postwar visions knew few limits. In fact, it may be difficult to grasp the tremendous optimism so many shared about the future. In particular, even the highways of the skyways promised a "sky's the limit" future of convenient air travel for the masses, with small aircraft the mode of travel for many. In this atmosphere, creating the vast infrastructure required for such a future offered opportunities rather than obstacles. *Greyhound Looks Ahead to Integrated Air-Bus Service*, published by Greyhound during World War II, offered one of these optimistic utopian visions for the future. "Long experience in transportation has given Greyhound a conviction of a growing need for the establishment of local air travel service. Such extension would make the benefits of air transportation readily available to millions of people in communities not now served by airlines. The wartime development of the helicopter, a revolutionary type of aircraft, has hastened the crystallization of Greyhound's plans."

In an effort to achieve this vision, Greyhound took practical steps. "On June 14, 1943, the Greyhound Corporation made application before the Civil Aeronautics Board for a Certification of Convenience and Necessity authorizing the operation of helicopters or similar aircraft over nearly 50,000 of the 63,000 miles of routes now traveled by Greyhound buses. An underlying principle of Greyhound's application is the *integration* of air service with bus service." According to the pamphlet, "Greyhound officials look to the helicopter as a means of giving America the same kind of efficient, flexible, frequent-stop service in the air that they now offer on the highway. The principal advantage of the helicopter is that it can take off or land without any forward motion, thus eliminating the necessity of large landing fields. This makes the craft ideal for service to smaller communities where construction and maintenance of large airports may not be feasible. Helicopter air buses could be landed on the roofs of many Greyhound terminals, close to business districts of towns and cities, or in adjacent lots." **[fig. 163]**

Greyhound addressed the issue of safety and, by inference, the ability to overcome the weather's impact on keeping to a schedule. Hindsight suggests the assurances were overly optimistic. "Because of its ability to maintain slow speeds, or even to hover motionless in the air, difficulties now encountered in foggy or overcast flying conditions are almost entirely eliminated. In the unlikely event of motor failure, the large rotor continues to revolve, acting as an airbrake and allowing the helicopter to settle slowly to earth.

Clearly anticipating the postwar prominence of air travel, Greyhound sought ways to capitalize on it as a bus company. "The volume of air travel has grown at a tremendous rate. Unquestionably the postwar expansion of air travel will be even more

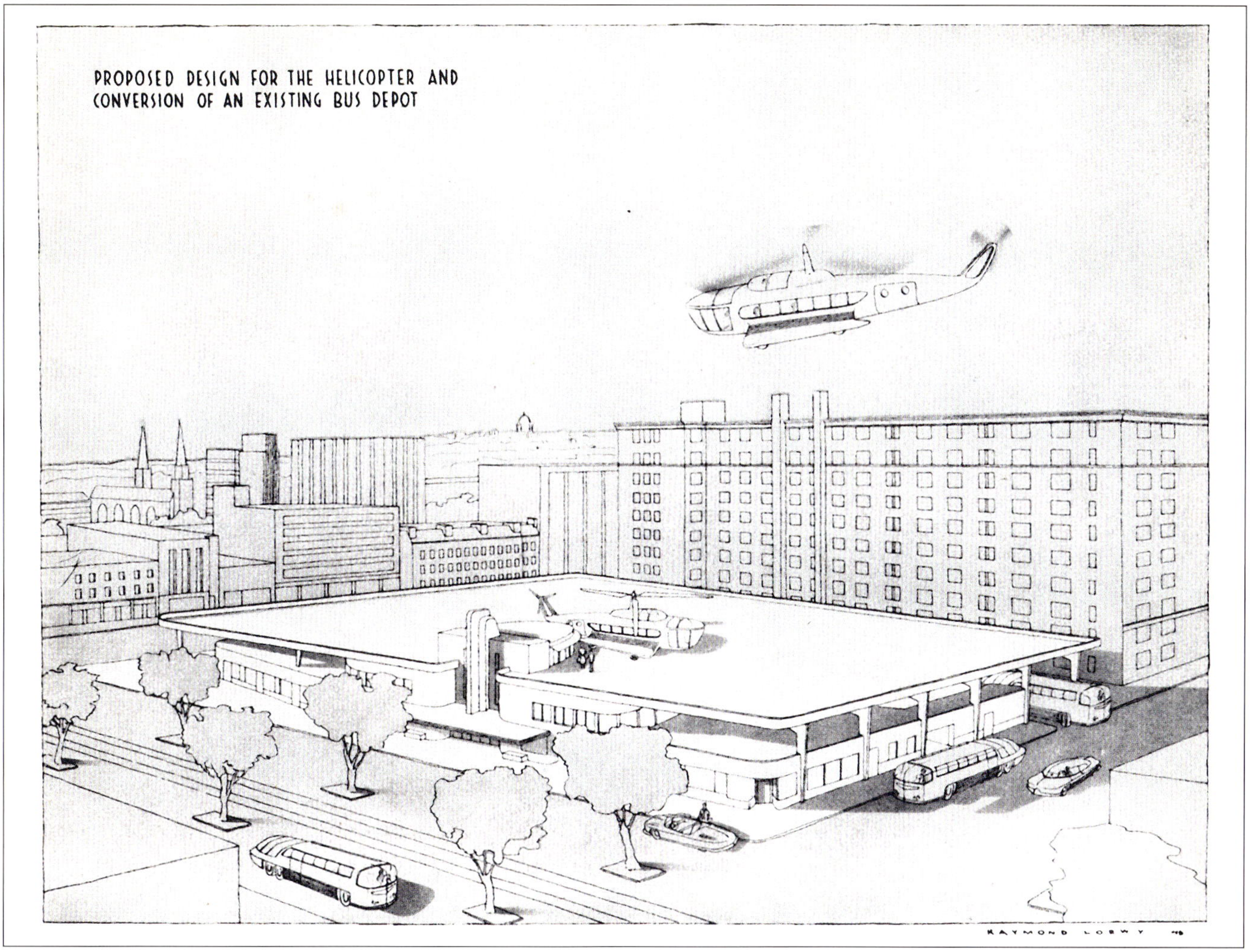

PROPOSED DESIGN FOR THE HELICOPTER AND
CONVERSION OF AN EXISTING BUS DEPOT

RAYMOND LOEWY

Fig. 163. Proposed Greyhound helicopter depot. *HML*

rapid." Greyhound also recognized the limited service airlines could offer to America's cities since airports would continue to serve major cities leaving most communities without direct air service. "Prior to Pearl Harbor, the nation's airlines provided direct service to only 240 of the 3,464 U.S. communities having a population of 2,500 or more. And of those 240 stops, only 40 were in cities of less than 10,000 population." Greyhound acknowledged the significant time spent traveling to a major airport, whether the traveler lived in a small town or rural area or even a "metropolitan center," thus negating the timesaving element of air travel. The air-bus service envisioned by Greyhound would provide a "faster form of transportation for trips up to 250 miles in length" and a "'feeder' system, making the through-travel services of the existing airlines more readily available to millions." Greyhound optimistically planned to have helicopter stops at 25- to 75-mile intervals with buses linking these locations to its larger network.

Fig. 164. Greyhound helicopter model. *HML*

Fig. 165. 1943 helicopter illustration. *HML*

Fig. 166. 1945 helicopter illustration. *HML*

Greyhound's efforts also included working with industrial designer Raymond Loewy to develop plans for a helicopter. Loewy developed drawings and scale models to illustrate the viability of the proposed helicopter. Greyhound provided the following caption for the illustration shown in its brochure: **[fig. 164]** "It is a far cry from the converted motorcars which carried the first bus passengers over America's highways, to the revolutionary helicopter. But each in its way symbolizes Greyhound's continuing ambition to provide ever-finer transportation." The proposed helicopter would accommodate 14 passengers. Loewy offered various design proposals for the Greyhound helicopter. **[fig. 165]** This rendering depicts a 1943 version, while this rendering **[fig. 166]** illustrates a 1945 design study. Loewy's firm also developed scale models of the proposed Greyhound helicopters. **[fig. 167]**

Fig. 167. Greyhound helicopter model. *HML*

This Loewy publicity image features the Greyhound helicopter superimposed over an aerial photograph of downtown St. Paul, Minnesota. **[fig. 168]** *Interiors* magazine used the illustration on its July 1945 cover.

Greyhound purchased two three-passenger Sikorsky helicopters, operating them on an experimental basis in 1946. In its 1947 *Annual Report*, however, Greyhound announced, "It now appears that it will be some years before the development of a helicopter of sufficient capacity for economical operation [...]. Greyhound has therefore abandoned its efforts to obtain authority to establish such service."

Also couched in terms of dreams, but more likely to see actual production, Greyhound planned new buses for the future. During the war, Greyhound advertisements promoted a glorious future of dreams come true, some including artist's renderings of a new Super-Coach designed by Raymond Loewy. Advertisements focusing on the future illustrated Greyhound's wartime intent to "maintain the strength and prestige of the Greyhound name against the time when competitive conditions will return." This November 18, 1944 *Saturday Evening Post* wartime advertisement declared, "Tomorrow's 'dream bus' is much more than a dream. It is shaping up today, in full scale models that will soon be translated into gleaming fluted metal, curved plastic glass, new type chairs built for long-trip relaxation—many features of comfort and efficiency we can't even talk about now. Super-Coaches like this are coming, sure as Victory." The advertisement also tapped into the

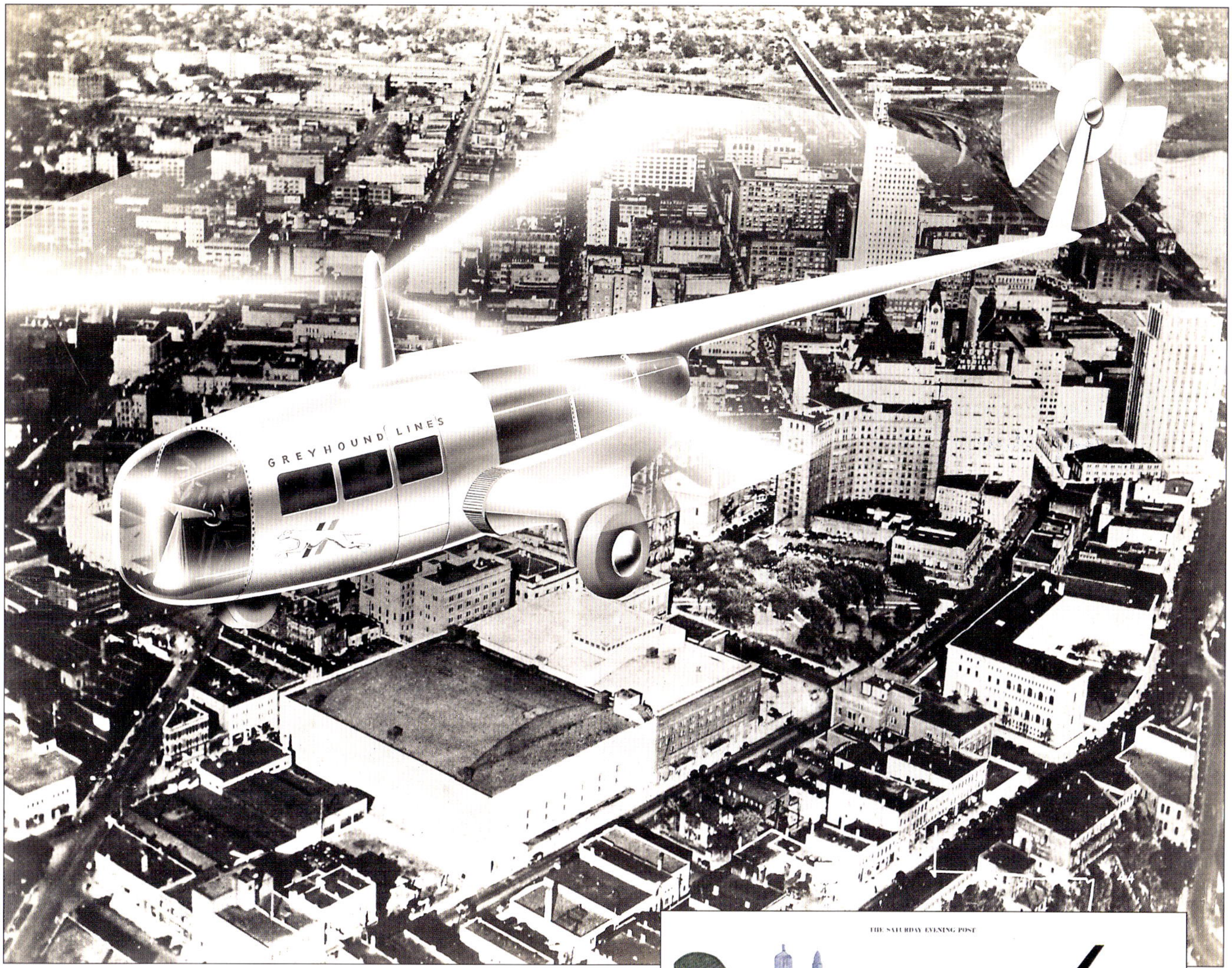

Fig. 168. Proposed helicopter, 1945. *HML*

theme so prominent before the war: The millions of returning "Service men and women (and travel-hungry millions at home)" will travel in these new dream buses "to see and enjoy 'This Amazing America.'" **[fig. 169]**

Greyhound advertisements also featured illustrations of the "NEW SUPER-COACH," assuring readers it was "more than a dream." This advertisement declared, "Just as American men and women have worked side by side in the shock of battle—as they have toiled together in the din of war plants—so they will one day re-discover the magnificent land for which they have fought…*still side-by-side!*" In the future, "millions will go by Greyhound." They will make their re-discovery trips by highway—because *only the highways* intimately reveal the lovely hidden places, the jeweled lakes and singing trout streams, the National Parks that are the heritage of every American." **[fig. 170]**

Fig. 169. *GBM*

Fig. 170. *GBM*

We're planning this around ***YOU!***

Greyhound architects and designers are looking straight at *you*, as they round out highway travel plans for the after-war days.

That means you men and women in your country's uniform—and everyone else who has worked earnestly in any job that has helped smash the Axis. It certainly means the millions of you who have taken wartime travel discomfort and crowding with a smile – like the good soldiers you are!

Greyhound terminals, stations and Post Houses (whether for big cities, smaller towns or pleasant wayside stops) are being planned around your personal travel needs—your desire for restful seating, appetizing food, bodily comfort, relaxation while waiting. In good time many of these terminals may even have helicopter landing decks.

You can be sure, too, that fine new motor coaches, built on tomorrow's faster, more luxurious lines, are now in the making—and that there'll be carefree sightseeing and pleasure tours to match.

Watch for all these—they're being planned around YOU.

GREYHOUND

Fig. 171. *GBM*

The Germans have surrendered, and while the war continues in the Pacific, peace seems possible soon. Considering the prospects for the postwar, readers of *Collier's* June 30, 1945 issue were told in "Stalin and World Unity" by Admiral William H. Standley, former Ambassador to the Soviet Union, that "Despite ups and downs in relations between our countries, Russia's overmastering desire is to get along with the U.S. and the world." Going through the magazine, reassured readers also encountered an advertisement offering all of Greyhound's postwar dreams. The young couple, emblematic of America's future, were told "Greyhound's architects and designers are looking at you, as they round out highway travel plans for the after-war years." A Raymond Loewy-designed helicopter approaches the landing deck on the terminal based on architect William Sudwick Arrasmith's 1942 proposal for Chicago. Raymond Loewy's "dream bus," the "Super-Coach," a common feature in Greyhound's late wartime advertisements, fills out the wish list. **[fig. 171]**

Declaring "These Dreams Will Come True" and depicting a postwar utopia, this wartime Greyhound advertisement described the dreams of returning soldiers and how it would play a role in making them come true. "When a fellow puts his uniform in mothballs and slips on those loose, easy civvies... that's comfort. When he and the lady he loves discover a velvet bank overlooking a river that runs all silver in the sunset—a place to dream those happy dreams...that's heaven! Hard months of war may lie ahead but, with final victory, Greyhound intends to help make a lot of those dreams come true for a lot of fighters—both in and out of uniform." **[fig. 172]**

As this advertisement indicates, Greyhound offered dreams of postwar opportunities to "Re-discover America" and to make these trips "by highway" in "luxurious new-type coaches" along with "better terminal and post-house facilities." It also reassured the reader that the new Super-Coaches "are more than a dream...they are shaping up right now."

Media reports covering Greyhound's new "Compartment Super Coach" began to appear in the late summer of 1944. Coverage usually featured this Raymond Loewy rendering, also used as the basis for advertising illustrations. **[fig. 173]** *Business Week*, September 2, 1944, reported, "Consolidated Vultee Aircraft Corp. will build three experimental models

Fig. 172. *MBS*

Fig. 173. Raymond Loewy design study. *GBM*

of the coaches in an effort to adapt the air-cooled aviation engine to the bus. General Motors, long-time builder of Greyhound buses, will construct three other experimental models which will be diesel-powered and will follow body construction methods recognized in the automotive industry." The article included the rendering, noting, "Raymond Loewy, industrial designer, styled the new buses [...]. He was aided by Greyhound engineers and by technical experts provided by the two manufacturers." Acknowledging the reality of war, the article asserted, "If wartime priorities can be licked, Greyhound hopes the experimental models will be completed early next year," with road tests to follow. Coverage based on Greyhound publicity material was widespread, appearing in newspapers throughout the country, including the *Cincinnati Post*, the *Winchester* [Illinois] *Times*, the *Princess Anne* [Maryland] *Herald*, and the *Hollywood* [Florida] *Herald*. The *Portland Oregonian*, November 26, 1944, also featured the commonly used Loewy rendering. The headline for the article, "Buses: The Highways' Magic Carpet for the Masses," reflected a key Greyhound goal, the democratization of travel.

Greyhound published its own brochure introducing the "revolutionary new type of motor coach" to the public, now called the "Highway Traveler." *The Highway Traveler*, Greyhound's promotional magazine (initially published as *The Greyhound Traveler* starting in 1929 and re-titled in 1931), became the basis for the name of the new bus. Greyhound used the Raymond Loewy rendering to illustrate the Highway Traveler brochure. "This strikingly different vehicle, which now incorporates important innovations never before seen in bus design, offers a pre-view of what highway travel may be like in the 1950s." The brochure continued, "The Highway Traveler is designed to open a new era in motor bus transportation, bringing to millions of bus travel patrons a host of vital service features they have long needed." Greyhound's long established goal—to make travel affordable and accessible to millions—is clearly evident. More importantly, the vision of future travel for the millions now included amenities formerly confined to the elite.

According to the brochure, the Highway Traveler, equipped with an air-suspension system, featured three separate passenger compartments designed "to provide the most spectacular opportunity for scenic travel ever offered on the nation's highways." Raymond Loewy's rendering provides a look at the initial concept. The brochure explained: "In the Fore Lounge, reached by a convenient inner stairway near the front of the Highway Traveler, six passengers enjoy an unequalled panoramic view through a virtual enclosure of expansive, non-glare windows,

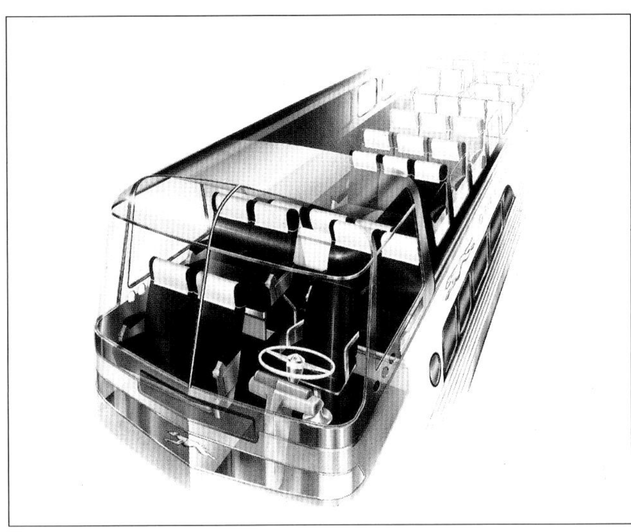

Fig. 174. Highway Traveler design study. *AACA*

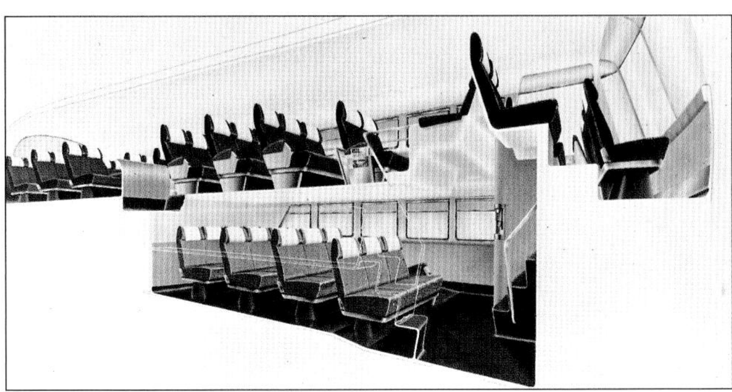

Fig. 175. Highway Traveler design study. *AACA*

windshields and transparent overdome. The driver is also seated in the Fore lounge. From his excellent vantage point he has a superb view of the highway for increased driving efficiency and safety [...]. The Terrace Lounge, also on the upper level but entirely separate from the Fore lounge, is wide and commodious and handsomely appointed. A few steps to this compartment open to the rear just off the main entrance way. The Terrace Lounge accommodates 31 passengers and treats them to superlative travel pleasure highlighted by the very finest scenic enjoyment, made possible by windows 50 percent larger than on present coaches." **[fig. 174]** While representing the latest in bus design, the Highway Traveler featured compartments reminiscent of the early Nite Coach designs introduced by Pickwick in the late 1920s.

Another Loewy rendering illustrates these features: "A single low step from the street gives easy access to the 13-passenger Sedan Lounge on the lower level. Here accommodations have been designed with a view toward providing a ride superior to that offered in the finest private automobiles." This compartment also offered "drinking facilities, a handy refrigerated cabinet and a completely equipped lavatory." The lavatory and food and beverage facilities in the Highway Traveler could mean faster service since "lost running time now resulting from frequent rest and meal stops might be substantially reduced." The three-compartment design suggests at least the possibility of a class-based fare structure. The brochure also offered this comment regarding seating: "Stationed at the door during loading periods, [the driver] can suggest and supervise appropriate seating." **[fig. 175]**

Twin air-cooled engines powered the experimental Highway Traveler. In normal operation "one engine propels the coach, while the other drives the generators and other accessory units. When extra power is needed, the auxiliary engine cuts in automatically." In addition, should one engine develop mechanical problems the other engine "can propel the bus and bring it to its destination." Each seat in the air-conditioned equipped bus featured radio speakers in the headrest. The driver selected "the two best stations" for passengers who only needed to touch buttons on their "lower seat edge" to listen, switch stations, or turn off the radio.

This new bus design for Greyhound was part of a larger context of long-term developments. In *Raymond Loewy: Designs for a Consumer Culture*, Glenn Porter asserts Loewy (1893-1986) "was at the center of the stage, particularly from the rise of consultant industrial design in the latter 1920s through the mid-1950s, when he reached his peak."

In designing helicopters and the Highway Traveler, Loewy contributed significantly to Greyhound's efforts to develop an image that conveyed modernity and promoted the desire to travel in style. Born in Paris, France, Loewy came to the United States in 1919, following the death of his parents in the influenza pandemic following World War I. Initially he worked in advertising in New York and by 1928 identified himself as a "commercial artist." According to Porter, "More than any other individual, he was responsible for convincing business of the importance of design." His talent, force of personality charm, energy, flair, his "Parisian air," and "genius" for self-promotion resulted in his preeminent status. Loewy's design work for Greyhound reflected what he labeled his "Contemporary American" style. Porter offered this definition: "It mixed the new with the traditional, and it created designs that suited American values—products and interiors were to be larger, more comfortable and convenient, constantly incorporating new technologies and novel materials but preferring to blend them with the old."

Loewy's design style, according to Porter, fit "an informal lifestyle in a frankly commercial, growth-oriented culture. It grew out of a worldview that particularly valued economic growth and the jobs implicit in growth. More goods and services, affordable by more and more people, lay at the heart of this vision." This design style clearly reflected the Greyhound philosophy presented in its advertisements. The newest design features would help encourage the further democratization of travel. Developing new styling for buses also complimented the entire travel experience, since travel is actually all about change. The act of movement is in itself change. As the bus moves down the road the scene out the window is ever changing. The road, upgraded and even rerouted, with new attractions just around the bend, also offers change. The vacation this year is to a new location compared to last year.

While visions of the future embodied revolutionary buses like the Highway Traveler, Greyhound had to deal with the present. The demands of years of war resulted in severely curtailed bus production as well as limited availability of replacement parts and a scarcity of materials for repairs to a fleet overburdened with the demands of extraordinary passenger loads. Because of their condition, replacement of these buses was essential. From a marketing standpoint, motoring on with the pre-war fleet was also unacceptable. Greyhound's promotion of revolutionary "Super-Coaches shaping up right now" created expectations about the future. Assuring the public that these dreams would come true was essential to Greyhound's reputation.

Postwar optimism confronted postwar reality. Shortages of manpower and materials continued during the re-conversion from wartime to peacetime production. Greyhound, however, was not alone in deferring significant change. Automobile and truck manufacturers, for example, while benefiting from pent-up demand, produced only slightly revised versions of prewar products, introducing significantly new models in 1949 or 1950. General Motors stylists developed proposals for restyled 1947 Silversides Super-Coaches. Two examples of rejected designs indicate the facelift nature of these

Fig. 176. Rejected facelift proposals, 1947 Silversides. *AACA*

proposals. **[fig. 176]** In all likelihood, Greyhound believed that instead of spending for these limited styling changes it would be more cost-effective to improve Silversides interiors and continue Highway Traveler development.

Despite the virtually identical exterior appearance—notice a revised front bumper—of the pre- and post-war Silversides, "new" was the key word in media coverage. "Greyhound Introduces New Bus," declared the Medford, Oregon, *Mail Tribune*. The Bluefield, West Virginia, *Telegraph* reported the "New Greyhound Coaches Glow in the Dark." The "glow" of the new bus resulted from the strips of "plastic glass film" applied to the front, rear, and sides as well as the Greyhound dog that "vividly reflects the headlights of other vehicles on the highways and makes the entire outline of the coach visible at night."

The extensive nationwide coverage of the glow-in-the-dark-coaches also included mention of the new interiors designed by Raymond Loewy. The *Eliza-*

Fig. 177. Restored 1947 Silversides. *AACA*

beth [West Virginia] *Journal*, with a very small circulation of 825, reported the "interior of the new 'Silversides' is decorated with metal, plastic, and natural wood. An entirely new color scheme, from light blue for the ceiling to a rich brown mohair for upholstery, presents a harmonious, dignified pattern. Improved interior lighting is another advancement in the new coach." Greyhound restored this 1947 Silversides for its Heritage Fleet. **[fig. 177]** A Greyhound folder declared, "Covered in fluted stainless steel and aluminum, and trimmed in Greyhound blue, the new coach presented a striking appearance." As "one of 1,800 diesel engine models built by General Motors that were added to the company's fleet after the war," the bus "marked the first time that [a portion of] a large fleet of buses was powered by diesel engines."

Not forgotten, the "romance of the road" returned in postwar guise. "America lives along the highway. From the first Indian tribes, such as the Six Nations of the Iroquois, who settled along the same buffalo path in order to be powerful—to present day Americans, who build homes near the road leading to the city in order to enjoy better living, highways have played the leading role in uniting the people of this Land." Greyhound offered this homage to the highway in *The*

Fig. 178. Promotional photo, 1947. *GBM*

Story of American Highways, the 1946 publication to assist teachers "to bring before the student the historical, social, and political meaning of that silver ribbon which joins his city, small town, or farm to the rest of the United States." The material offered perspectives on the significance of highways in the development of the United States and an explanation of their

Fig. 179. *MBS*

Fig. 180. *MBS*

Fig. 181. *MBS*

importance in the "new era" of postwar highway construction. Fundamental features of postwar visions for many, including Greyhound, were various expressions of brotherhood and social harmony included in the materials. "The highways of today help to keep America united" by bringing people closer together, making a "happier 'American family.'" **[fig. 178]**

The teaching material also explained the new highways would produce significant benefits. "Highway routes through the cities will be made 'non-stop,' by building them above or below ground. New highways mean new strength for America. With this network of roads that will speed up highway travel, the United States Army will be able to rush troops to any shore in the Nation if a foreign attack should occur. The new highways will allow speeds of 70 miles an hour in the country and 45 miles an hour in the city—in complete safety." In addition, "The new highways mean wealth for America." Offering a somewhat dated scenario, the text proclaimed, "The farmer will no longer have to struggle in hub-deep mud to carry his crops to market." In a more relevant example, Greyhound asserted the new highways also

Fig. 182. *GBM*

promised money-saving "greater speed" for manufacturers and distributors.

The new highways promised something else—something the ordinary American could attain. "Perhaps the first result of the new highways will appear as the greatest surge of pleasure travel in history. It has been only recently that Americans began to realize the scenic pleasure that lies in the beauty-lined highways of their Land. The Greyhound System has expressed this truth in its advertising campaign, "Only by Highway." *The Story of American Highways* clearly reflected the optimism of most Americans following the war. The final paragraph proclaimed that a better life is to come following years of depression and war. "The meaning of new highways is, therefore, better, happier living. With this great stride in our way of life, we can enjoy the benefits of this Land more easily, understand the people of our Nation more readily...and we can live, work, and play in greater comfort and increasing pleasure."

Greyhound's "Only by Highway" advertising campaign, referred to in *The Story of American Highways,* focused on the "magnificent corridors of the Redwood Highway" as an example of the "wayside wonders" the Greyhound traveler could see "close up!" In the lower right-hand corner, the reader is encouraged to "Hear your favorite radio and screen stars sing and play 'Love on a Greyhound Bus' from the coming MGM picture 'NO LEAVE—NO LOVE'—starring Van Johnson, with Pat Kirkwood, Keenan Wynn, Marie Wilson, Guy Lombardo, Xavier Cugat. This hit song is on records now, with your favorite band." **[fig. 179]** Other examples featured U.S. Highway 1 along the New England Coast **[fig. 180]** and an attractive mother and daughter who have followed "the sun to winter fun." **[fig. 181]**

Set to music, some postwar dreams recast the meaning of romance for the Greyhound traveler. *Time*, April 14, 1947, declared it was a "New Day for the Hound." The article began with words from "Love on a Greyhound Bus," highlighted in the "Only by Highway" advertisement. **[fig. 182]**

Soon the sun disappeared from view,
The stars came out like they always do,
Then I cuddled up close to you,
And we both fell in love on a Greyhound Bus'
That's us—in love on a Greyhound Bus...."

In what would be a stretch for most, *Time* used the song and the theme of romance as an opportunity to promote the new Silversides buses ordered by Greyhound, noting they would offer, "More comforts for Cupid." *Time* declared, "In tune with this popular song," the "Greyhound Corp. plans to carry romance and its paying customers more comfortably than ever before. Soon Greyhound, world's biggest intercity bus company, will put into operation the first of 1,500 new 37-passenger buses, first Greyhound replacement since 1942. The new aluminum buses, designed by Raymond Loewy Associates and costing $38 million, are air-conditioned and contain such gadgets as a seat which is 'shaped to the human form.'"

Time noted the role of Greyhound President Orville Caesar in these changes. "Though the Hound is already elephant-sized, Caesar, 54, plans to keep it right on growing. He now has in the works a $20 million project for new terminals, at New York, Chicago, and San Francisco, along with garages, restaurants and comfort stations." The most important news dealt with the Highway Traveler. Featuring Loewy's rendering, the article explained "Caesar has spent half a million dollars building an experimental double-decker bus for long haul, express runs. Worked out with designer [Raymond] Loewy, it will be only 18 inches higher than present buses and no longer. But the tricky new seat arrangement will permit 13 more passengers to be carried, 50 *v.* 37 in present buses. It also has a washroom, toilet, water cooler, may even carry a hostess. The driver sits in a special clearview compartment between the two decks."

Greyhound finally turned dreams into reality in the spring of 1948, unveiling the long promised experimental Highway Traveler. **[fig. 182]** The *Lima* [Ohio] *News*, April 1, 1948, declared, "Greyhound Unveils 'Dream' Bus at Terminal Opening." As with other newspapers, the *News* began its account with reference to a key passenger amenity, a "built-in toilet," proclaiming "The day of the begrimed bus traveler, the person who dashes madly for a rest room at every bus stop apparently is over." The introduction of the Highway Traveler occurred at the March 31st grand opening of the new terminal in Cleveland, billed as the "world's biggest, most comfortable bus terminal." The extensive national coverage emphasized the important role of "Raymond Loewy Associates, noted industrial designers" in the development of the "body and interior layout." In its coverage, the

Fig. 182. 1948 Highway Traveler. *AACA*

Fig. 183. Highway Traveler and a Silversides. *MBS*

Cleveland [Ohio] *News* offered a side-by-side comparison with the postwar Silversides Super-Coach and the experimental Highway Traveler. Other newspapers, including the *Marietta* [Ohio] *Times,* explained the new bus had begun road testing "over every type of terrain and in every climate," but "Greyhound did not expect the busses to be on the roads in quantity before 1950." This scene illustrates the Highway Traveler's startling design departure from current automobiles and the Silversides Super-Coach, the mainstay of Greyhound's fleet for the foreseeable future. [**fig. 183**]

Fig. 184. *MBS*

Fig. 185. *MBS*

Despite the delays in the production of the promised Highway Traveler, Greyhound advertising offered assurances that dreams and enchantment did await the Greyhound traveler. Re-introducing the Amazing America Tours initially promoted in the 1930s and the prewar-1940s, Greyhound's postwar publicity noted these tours were under the direction of Greyhound Highway Tours, Inc., and available through Greyhound Travel Bureaus or local Greyhound agents. **[fig. 184]** With the war over, the romance of the road could return.

While Greyhound advertising featured images of new modern highways and unimpeded journeys, actual travel in the late 1940s could also involve very different experiences. "Mountain Bus Driver," by Don Wharton, appeared in the November 1948 issue of *Holiday*, America's premiere travel magazine. Wharton traveled with Greyhound driver Johnnie Jones on the ride from Winston Salem, North Carolina, to Charleston, West Virginia, "267 miles across the mountains." Wharton explains the bus must complete the trip on narrow winding two-lane roads often waiting to pass slower moving trucks and automobiles. "As Johnnie swings the bus around horseshoe curves, higher and higher, a hush falls over the passengers. Those who speak at all talk in low tones." After a lunch stop, "Johnnie is back on the highway, winding past old log cabins with brick chimneys and over hazardous one-way bridges. To reach Bluefield, in West Virginia he must take the bus over three mountains." Johnnie declares, "You ought to make this trip with me in the winter; ice all through here, snowdrifts sometimes twice as high as the bus." Wharton notes that a discharged soldier gets out of the bus, "The swishing around the mountain has made him sick." The message to the traveler is that the ride is without a traffic related incident, a testament to the skill of Johnnie Johnson, who has logged 1,093,000 accident free miles and thus a lesson for those who want to travel by bus.

Continuing the themes of comfort, convenience, and value/economy used to encourage travel prior to World War II, Greyhound published *America Celebrates: A travel map of Festivals, Pageants and Special Events reached by...Greyhound* in 1949. **[fig. 185]** Greyhound promised, "Travel in low-cost luxury to any of the Nation's Celebrations." Among the celebrations highlighted included the Berkshire Music Festivals, Tanglewood, Massachusetts; the Christmas Regatta, Newport-Balboa Harbor, California; the Latin-America Festival, Tampa, Florida; the

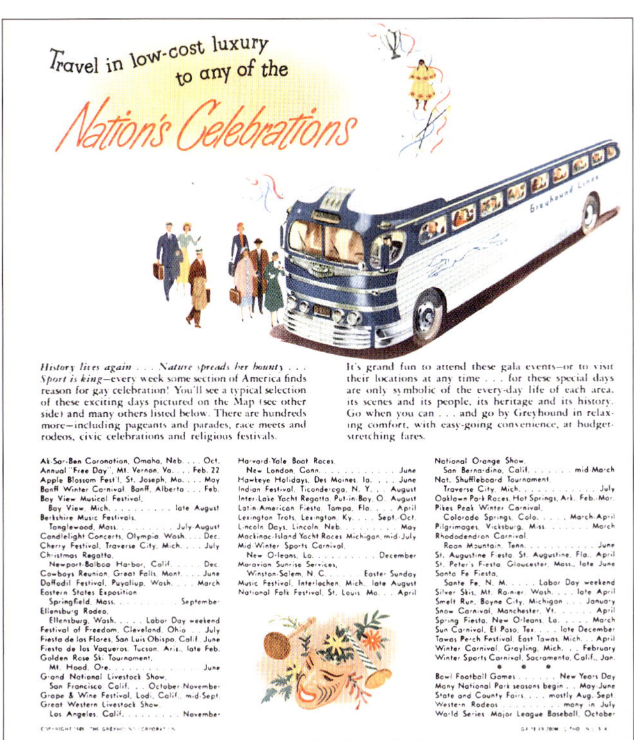

Fig. 186. *MBS*

Fig. 187. *MBS*

National Shuffleboard Tournament, Traverse City, Michigan; the Smelt Run, Boyne City, Michigan; and the Snow Carnival, Manchester, Vermont. The brochure declared, "It's grand fun to attend these gala events—or to visit their locations anytime…for these special days are only symbolic of the every-day life of each area, its scenes and its people, its heritage and its history. Go when you can…and go by Greyhound in relaxing comfort, with easy-going convenience, at budget-stretching fares." **[fig. 186]**

While the destination was important, the means to get there continued as a crucial facet of Greyhound's advertising promotions. Well dressed, middle class "congenial, Greyhound passengers relax, nap, enjoy the passing scene" because "when you step aboard a Greyhound, [you] sink back into one of the deeply cushioned, body-contoured chairs… you enjoy the most restful ride you've ever had! It's smoother, more relaxing than even the costliest private limousine." The bus offered a "long wheelbase, perfected springing; skillfully designed seats of foam rubber; adjustable footrests; controlled temperature, efficient ventilation; Solex safety glass windows, adjustable shades, focused lighting; [and] inside luggage racks." These well-engineered buses and the "highly-trained drivers" provided the requisite safety. **[fig. 187]**

Other Greyhound brochures indicated the drivers were also part of an entire work force "known for their courtesy." Brochures emphasized the terminals are located right in the heart of major cities and offer easy access to downtown theater, shopping, and business districts. Since the war Greyhound has constructed many newer, finer terminals with complete ticket and information facilities—plus every modern convenience, from restaurants, rest rooms and baggage lockers to news stands, showers, and barber shops." In addition to the major terminals, Greyhound explained, "You can generally stop at any city, any town or cross-roads community, and even at farm gates en route." Greyhound also assured value with fares "lower than any other form of transportation. Greyhound costs only a fraction as much as driving your own car—often saves enough for extra vacation days or extra trips."

In 1949, author Don Eddy traveled on a cross-country 3,000-mile tour via Greyhound Silversides Super-Coach. *American Magazine* published his account, "I'm a Vacation Bus Rider," in its July 1950 issue. Eddy indicated his initial response to the assignment: "To be honest with you, I sort of dreaded it." However, after the trip he declared, "I was never uncomfortable, never shoved around, never too cold or too warm, never annoyed. It was

Fig. 188. *Author's Collection*

the most restful [trip] I ever made. It was infinitely easier, considerably cheaper, just as fast as driving my own car. To me, an experienced traveler, it was a revelation. To tell the truth, what started as a job turned out to be a real vacation, one of the most enjoyable I ever had. From now on, I'm a confirmed vacation bus rider." Eddy's observations reflected themes common to Greyhound advertising. "Don't worry about the bus driver. He had to be practically a genius to get the job in the first place." In addition, "Bus stations nearly always are in the center of town." Also, "There is exactly the amount of camaraderie on a cross-country bus that you care to have." The low cost of the travel proved a very pleasant surprise. Eddy did offer a mixed review of food and restrooms. Noting they "worry bus companies most," he opined, "On my trip, I never had a bad meal. Restrooms, however, can stand a lot of improvement. The worst are in small towns."

In the fall of 1949, this advertisement, appealing to a variety of travelers, featured five tableaux. Using long established romance of the road rhetoric, the advertisement also acknowledged the concerns of the cost conscious. "This is Take-a-Trip Time all over America to answer the call of open highways, of falling leaves, of golden haze and drifting wood smoke! Greyhound alone can give you supreme enjoyment of Fall and Winter trips—not only because it follows these pleasant highways, but because it costs far less per mile than any other kind of travel." **[fig. 188]**

Ice Follies

In 1956, one of America's premiere ice-skating shows looked back in celebration of its 20th Anniversary. In November 1936, the 23-member troupe of the Shipstads and Johnson Ice Follies assembled at the corner of University Avenue and Snelling Avenue in St. Paul, Minnesota, to board a Greyhound bus for Tulsa, Oklahoma. The bus performed flawlessly, but for the less determined the trip might have resulted in the end of dreams. A polio outbreak severely limited attendance in Tulsa, with the cast nearly outnumbering customers for the first performance. The next two performances saw less than 500 customers. The troupe quickly left Tulsa amidst rumors of possible quarantine. A severe blizzard in Kansas City kept customers away and business in St. Louis also proved disappointing. The performances in Philadelphia proved to be the key to success. Impressed with the show, agents from major venues throughout the East booked the show.

The 1946 Ice Follies program sold at performances commemorated the organization's Tenth Anniversary with a photograph of the troupe on the Greyhound bus bound for Tulsa.

As part of its 20th Anniversary celebration, the Ice Follies tracked down the bus they took on that 1936 trip. No longer owned by Greyhound, a private owner used the bus for round trips from Rapid City, South Dakota, to Mount Rushmore. Greyhound personnel helped locate the bus. The Ice Follies refurbished the bus and used it to transport founders Eddie and Roy Shipstad and Oscar Johnson and a "flock of movie stars from Chasens Restaurant to the Pan Pacific Auditorium for the World Premier" of the 1956 Ice Follies.

Author's Collection

Greyhound's Roadside: 1945-1954

The war is over and the hungry travelers passing through Kentland, Indiana, south of Hammond, Indiana, have stopped at this Post House, one of 66 in operation in 1946. *AACA*

Along the Pacific coast on U.S. Highway 101, Newport, Oregon, offered travelers in 1947 the convenience of a depot and the Bay Way Café. Greyhound also operated ninety-eight Post House restaurants in 1947. *AACA*

Located on famous Highway 61 north of the Twin Cities of St. Paul, and Minneapolis, Minnesota, at Hinckley, Minnesota, was Tobie's, a local landmark that while much altered, still serves travelers today—just off the interstate exit. *GBM*

Approximately fifty miles west of Nashville, Waverly, Tennessee, provided this Streamline Moderne Post House for travelers. *GBM*

Greyhound travelers on the "Mother Road," Route 66, bound for Albuquerque, New Mexico, pause for a meal at the Lebanon, Missouri, Post House. *GBM*

The staff of Greyhound's Lima, Ohio, Post House located in the Greyhound Terminal designed by architect W. R. Arrasmith, poses for a Grand Opening Day publicity photograph in 1949. *GBM*

Appetizers
Fruit Cocktail .15
Grapefruit Juice .10
Tomato Juice .10
Orange Juice .10
Seafood Cocktail .35

Soup
Oyster Bisque Parisienne .20

Special of the Day
Oyster Bisque Parisienne
Roast Turkey with Almond Celery Stuffing
Cranberry Sauce
Buttered Green Peas
Snow Flake Potatoes — Chef's Salad — Beverage
Roll and Butter — Tutti Frutti Short Cake
$1.10

1. Baked Filet of White Fish
Lemon Butter, Chef's Salad, Parsley Potatoes
Beverage — Roll and Butter .85
2. Baked Ham, Pineapple Sauce
Mashed Yams, Green Peas, Beverage
Roll and Butter .80
3. Spaghetti Milanaise
Parmesan Cheese, Chef's Salad
Beverage — Roll and Butter .70
4. Casserole of Lamb Stew
Chef's Salad .65

Carving Table
Hot Corned Beef .35
Roast Beef .35
— Served on Rye Bread —

Children's Special
Peanut Butter Sandwich — or
Chicken Salad Sandwich — Cup of Soup
and Dessert .25

Salads
Chicken Salad with Tomatoes,
Saratoga Chips, Sweet Pickle .75
Waldorf Salad .20
Chef's Tossed Salad .15

Desserts
Tutti Frutti Short Cake .25
Pie or Layer Cake .15
Fruit Jello .10
Ice Cream .10

Beverages
Greyhound Post House Coffee .10
Grade "A" Milk, Individual Bottle .15
Pot of Tea .10

Opening Day • Chicago

This photograph illustrates the menu for the Chicago grand opening. *GBM*

In October 1949, Greyhound opened its new depot and Post House restaurant in Chicago, Illinois. *GBM*

In 1947, Greyhound established a resort on one of the islands in the Florida Keys. Located 90 miles from Miami and 69 miles from Key West, and approximately 10 miles south of Craig, Greyhound Key featured a Post House and a series of guest cottages. Utilizing long established romance-of-the-road rhetoric, Greyhound promotional material declared, "Enjoy your own private Pleasure Island. You'll discover a new vacation experience when you come to Greyhound Key… an island paradise with a past that lends enchantment to your visit. For the vacation of tropical romance and relaxation, there's no place quite like Greyhound Key." *GBM*

Fig. 189. Senicruiser design study. *MBS*

In mid-1949, Greyhound offered a prophetic vision of the future. Unlike the experimental Highway Traveler, the distinctive Scenicruiser, also initially experimental, would become one of Greyhound's most famous buses. This undated Raymond Loewy Associates rendering indicates an earlier concept based on the experimental two-axle Highway Traveler. **[fig. 189]** The *Boston* [Massachusetts] *Globe*, July 3, 1949 featured this widely used photograph for its coverage. **[fig. 190]** The *Globe* reported, "The Scenicruiser, a revolutionary type of motor bus which will set standards of luxury in highway travel never before realized, began tests [on July 2] for the Greyhound Lines." Built by "Greyhound engineers and mechanics in the Chicago plant of Greyhound Motors and Supply Co.," the Scenicruiser project involved the "active cooperation and assistance of Raymond Loewy Associates, industrial designers, and the styling section of General Motors." The *Paris* [Tennessee] *Parisian* noted that such collaboration "ought to guarantee a snazzy-looking vehicle." **[fig. 191]**

The extensive coverage of the experimental dual rear axle Scenicriuser emphasized the "most striking innovation," the raised rear level seating 33 passengers. The *Wall Street Journal*, reminiscent of the 1930s buses featuring railroad car features, suggested this feature was "on the order of the 'vista dome' coaches of some railroads." The *Washington* [D.C.] *Pathfinder* illustrated its coverage of the "Glass-Domed Coach" with this photograph and explanation. **[fig. 192]** "At the rear is a lounge with leather-upholstered seats."

Fig. 190. 1949 Senicruiser test model. *MBS*

Fig. 191. 1949 Senicruiser test model. *AACA*

Fig. 192. Senicruiser rear lounge. *HML*

Fig. 193. Senicruiser interior. *GBM*

This is the view looking forward from the lounge area of the experimental concept model. **[fig. 193]** The design also provided a 10-passenger forward deck with seating for the driver in a position closer to the road compared to the Highway Traveler. Despite its 50-foot length, five feet longer than conventional buses, the 43-passenger Scenicriuser carried seven less passengers than the Highway Traveler. **[fig. 194]** This Raymond Loewy Associates "X-Ray" drawing illustrates the interior.

While undergoing testing, Greyhound exhibited the Scenicruiser at a variety of locations throughout the United States and Canada including Gladstone, Michigan; San Francisco and Oakland, California; New Orleans, Louisiana; Atlanta, Georgia; Evansville, Indiana; and Montreal, Canada. The local newspapers, relying on Greyhound publicity, emphasized the same features. Readers learned about the "double-glazed big windows" that comprised "more than 90 percent of the side structure above the seat level," the "broad rooflights of special safety glass permitting a sky view for passengers," the "lavatory, drinking fountain, two-way radio, and public address system." **[fig. 195]** None of the accounts mentioned the already famous Silversides-inspired Alumilite body covering.

Some aspects of the Scenicruiser design changed during testing. By August 29, 1951, Greyhound provided altered photographs for publicity. This photograph illustrates the elimination of the cowling enclosed destination sign above the windshield. **[fig. 196]** Greyhound's brochure to acquaint the traveling public with its "NEW Revolutionary Scenicruiser" also utilized this photograph as the basis for the cover illustration. **[fig. 197]**

The promotion of futuristic buses was an essential element in Greyhound's efforts to cast itself as a leader in transportation innovation. Greyhound also benefited from publicity about travel in the present. Motion pictures featuring Greyhound buses date back to 1934 and "It Happened One Night," starring Clark Gable and Claudette Colbert. The April 1951 *Atlantic Courier*, Atlantic Greyhound's in-house

Fig. 194. Senicruiser design study. *HML*

Fig. 195. Senicruiser under testing. *MBS*

publication, covered the RKO motion picture, "Two Tickets to Broadway," starring Gloria DeHaven, Ann Miller, Barbara Lawrence, Janet Leigh, and Tony Martin. The film featured Greyhound Silversides Super-Coaches in several scenes. According to the *Courier*, "The use of Greyhound buses for transportation is a definite part of the plot of the picture."

While spectacular and designed to express the utopian visions prominent in the 1930s and 1940s, Greyhound did not intend the Scenicruiser to be the major component of its fleet. As Scenicruiser development continued, Greyhound unveiled the production version of the Highway Traveler. **[fig. 198]** Not to be confused with the three deck experimental model, first introduced in Greyhound advertising during World War II, Greyhound intended this Highway Traveler to replace the heart of its fleet, the

Fig. 196. 1951 Senicruiser. *MBS*

Fig. 197. *MBS*

Silversides Super-Coach. Introduced in 1953, the design configuration of this Highway Traveler dates back to the 1935 X-1 and the production models that it spawned—the first Super-Coaches. As with these earlier models, the new Highway Traveler featured an elevated seating deck over the baggage compartments with engines located at the rear.

Retaining a version of the Silversides external body panels, the bus featured a front-end design based on the experimental Scenicruiser, and would become virtually identical to the production version. As noted in press coverage, in sharp contrast to previous designs, the Highway Traveler featured, as the *Charleston* [West Virginia] *Gazette*, June 14, 1953 reported, "huge picture windows—so big that only four are needed for each side," making "sightseeing doubly exciting and enjoyable." Continuing, the article explained "The four double windows, six feet in length, gives the coach a glass area 53.7 percent greater than in previous models. These windows are heat resistant safety glass, tinted green to cut sun glare by half." **[fig. 199]** The *Natchez* [Mississippi] *Times*, May 12, 1953 lead off its report declaring, "The Greatest advance in motor bus history introduced in

Fig. 198. 1953 Highway Traveler. *GBM*

Fig. 199. 1953 Highway Traveler. *AACA*

this coach is an air suspension system, heralded as the 'new ride,' which completely eliminates metal leaf springs. Compressed air, held captive in eight heavy, flexible air bellows, two to each wheel, silently and efficiently absorbs all types of road shock. A unique feature of the air suspension system is that leveling valves act to keep the coach body constantly level on curves or despite changes in the weight of the load carried."

"Power steering, noted the *Amboy* [Minnesota] *Herald*, May 22, 1953, "which has been an extra cost accessory on the most expensive automobiles for the past year, is an exclusive Greyhound feature." The August 11, 1953, *Santa Monica* [California] *Outlook* account of the interior mirrored most others. "The interior styling of the new bus, in pastel tones of tan and brown, was created for Greyhound by Raymond Loewy and Associates. An improved type of indi-

Fig. 200. Highway Traveler interior. *AACA*

Fig. 201. Promotional photo, 1956. *GBM*

vidually-controlled reclining seats is an important comfort feature for passengers. Seat areas, made of foam rubber, are wider and backs are 'dished' to give each passenger privacy and freedom from crowding." **[fig. 200]** The heating and air conditioning systems received positive comments in all accounts.

Promotional efforts by Greyhound utilized the Highway Traveler to promote a 1950s vision of the romance of the road. The majestic landscape featuring the Golden Gate Bridge **[fig. 201]** and the close-up featuring a poolside couple **[fig. 202]** offer two tableaus romanticizing travel.

Meanwhile, as the experimental version of the Scenicruiser toured the country undergoing testing and appearing for promotional exhibits, development of the production version continued. These 1953 mock-ups illustrate a phase in that process. **[fig.**

Fig. 202. Promotional photo, 1954. *GBM*

Fig. 203. Two views of the Senicruiser mock-up, 1953. *AACA*

203] Despite the introduction of the Highway Traveler, it was the Scenicruiser that fulfilled the utopian dreams Greyhound promised for revolutionary postwar motor coaches. The July 27, 1954 issue of the *Cheyenne* [Wyoming] *State Tribune and State Leader* announced this development with a press agent's hyperbole. "July 14th marked the beginning of a new era in highway travel. On that date, in Pontiac, Michigan, the first Greyhound Scenicruiser rolled off the General Motors production line." The article offered this assessment: "Setting new standards of highway travel luxury, the revolutionary new Scenicruiser represents the most important milestone in bus travel in the last 25 years." **[fig. 204]**

Despite the extensive coverage of the experimental Scenicruiser, media coverage generally presented the production Scenicruiser as if the experimental version had never existed, with features introduced on the 1953 Highway Traveler and included on the Scenicruiser offered as new innovations. Coverage usually indicated, "Fifteen years planning, design, and experimentation by the Greyhound Corp. went into the production of today's Scenicruiser" without

Fig. 204. 1954 Senicruiser. *GBM*

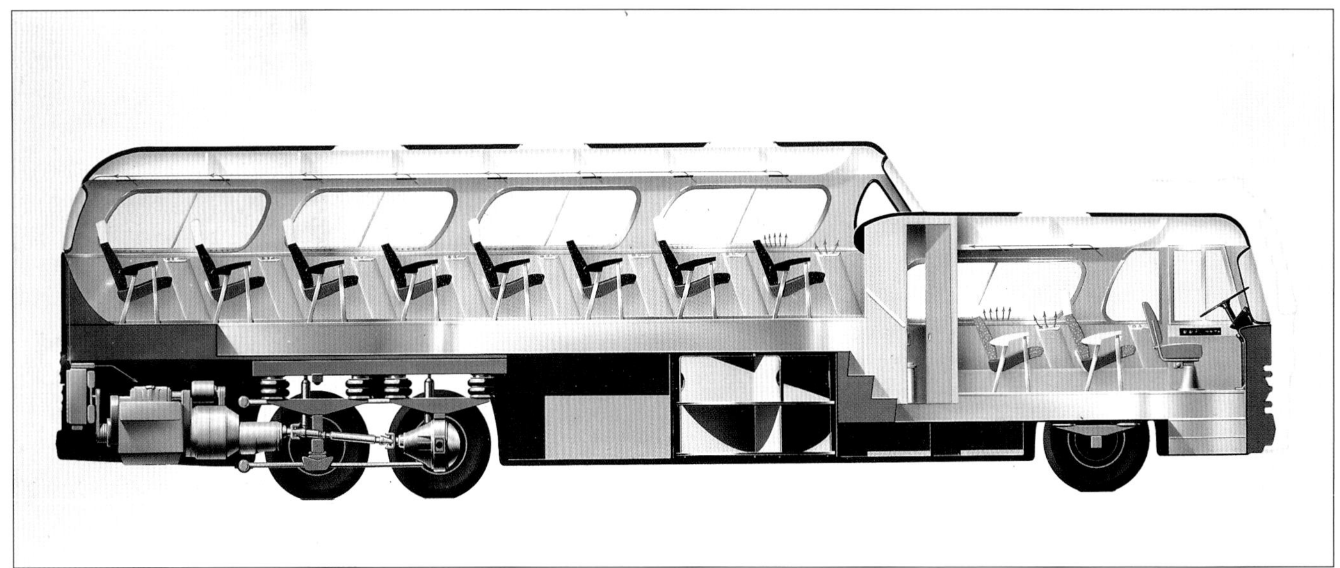

Fig. 205. Senicruiser X-ray view. *MBS*

mentioning the prototype. One of the exceptions, the *Dallas* [Texas] *News*, October 10, 1954 covered "Tomorrow's bus today," noting "Two experimental models, GX-1 and GX-2 went through cycles of service-improvement to result in today's double-decker." The *News* offered this explanation of the significance of the new bus: The "fabulous new double-deck Scenicruiser climaxes a two months tour over the Southwest to take its place among other engineering marvels of our age at the State Fair of Texas." The article also featured this widely used "X-Ray view." **[fig. 205]** Compare this with the experimental version **(fig. 194, page 126)**. Like the experimental prototype, the production Scenicruiser featured a lavatory, seating for 43 (with 33 on the upper level and 10 on the lower level behind the driver), and a 40-foot

Fig. 206. Senicruiser publicity photos, 1955. *MBS*

Fig. 207. *MBS*

Fig. 208. *GBM*

Fig. 209. *GBM*

length. In contrast, the production model featured two diesel engines instead of one (twin air-cooled engines powered the experimental Highway Traveler), and an air suspension system first introduced on the 1953 Highway Traveler, compared to metal springs on the experimental Scenicruiser. Like the Highway Traveler, the Scenicruiser featured power steering as well as power brakes.

Media coverage always acknowledged the involvement of Raymond Loewy Associates. Typical is this from the *San Antonio* [Texas] *News*, January 5, 1955: "Interior styling is by Raymond Loewy Associates and uses a motif of smart, modern designs and colors." Other accounts stressed the "fine fabrics in bright colors" and the "comfort of deep foam rubber reclining easy chairs with increased leg room and adjustable footrests." Greyhound publicity photographs provide views of the Scenicruiser's lower level lavatory **[fig. 206]** and upper level passenger seating area. **[fig. 207]** This image shows passengers looking out the much touted lower level "six-foot 'picture' window." **[fig. 208]** In its September 23, 1954 edition, the *Ashland* [Wisconsin] *Press* featured this photograph, adding, "375 people made personal

Fig. 210. *GBM*

Fig. 211. *GBM*

inspections of the interior during its 50 minute stop at the Bus Depot." [**fig. 209**]

The "face" of Greyhound was changing. The distinctively designed Highway Traveler and Scenicruiser offered a new look—embodiments of the wartime utopian vision that assured Americans that "Tomorrow's 'dream bus' is much more than a dream. It is shaping up today, in full scale models that will soon be translated into gleaming fluted metal, curved plastic glass, new type chairs built for long-trip relaxation—many features of comfort and efficiency we can't even talk about now." Greyhound's advertising, reflecting a changing style, also offered a new look. While a subjective judgment—the "romance of the road" is ultimately in the mind of the beholder—Greyhound's advertising seems less romanticized. Artist's illustrations, the prominent feature of Greyhound advertisements from the 1930s and 1940s, increasingly gave way to photography, a medium more realistic and hence less subjective and romantic. Compare the 1938 advertisement [**fig. 210**] that invited the traveler to "Ride With Us *in this* $20,000 automobile," with this 1953 version [**fig. 211**] encouraging a ride in the "$33,000 Highway Traveler that 'floats on cushions of air.'"

Fig. 212. *GBM*

If aspects of the artistic style were less romantic, the messages continued to rely on long-established appeals to the thrill and excitement of travel—the romance of the road. As in the 1930s and 1940s, Greyhound encouraged travel for women. Declaring, "Greyhound brings America a New Era of Travel!" this October 16, 1954 *Saturday Evening Post* advertisement featured "the recently chosen Mrs. America for 1955," the "charming Wanda Jennings." The epitome of 1950s middle class fashion with her suit, gloves, pillbox hat with veil, and simulated alligator skin overnight bag, Mrs. America declares, "It's a thrilling travel experience to ride either of these wonderful coaches!" She represented "the millions of 'Mrs. Americas' who especially appreciate the tasteful appointments, the relaxed body comfort, the panoramic sightseeing, found only in Greyhound's *Scenicruiser* and *Highway Traveler* buses." While married she offered an image of the self-reliant, independent woman. The advertisement's emphasis is on the thrill that comes from riding these buses with "Air Suspension Ride... huge picture windows...[and] air conditioning." Unlike earlier advertising, a romantic destination is implicit—the reader can only imagine that, as one of the millions of "Mrs. Americas," their "thrilling travel experience" will be to someplace romantic. **[fig. 212]**

Mrs. America, Wanda Jennings, participated in the official Presentation Ceremony, July 14, 1954. Greyhound's news release explained. "When the first Scenicruiser came off the production line it was christened by 'Mrs. America,' Wanda Jennings of St. Louis, and 'presented' to her by Greyhound President Orville S. Caesar. He did this to symbolize the fact that he was presenting the special new bus to American women everywhere." As a "Parade of Historical Buses built by GMC Truck and Coach Division and its predecessor, Yellow Truck and Coach Manufacturing Co." passed in review, attendees heard this: "And now finally here is the beautiful new Scenicriuser, which we believe will bring about a new age in highway travel."

GREYHOUND TERMINAL ALBUM: 1945-1954

Following the war, Greyhound renewed its program of terminal construction. Following the 1948 Cleveland, Ohio, terminal, designs increasingly reflected more angular design motifs, foreshadowed in the 1942 Baltimore terminal. Frank E. Wrenick, in his study of Greyhound terminal design asserted, "After the war there was a distinct shift in the architectural taste of the nation and Streamline Moderne with its curvilinear lines was replaced by a more crisp avant-garde style." However, the designs are hardly "avant-garde," continuing to embody modernism.

The September 1949, *Bus Transportation* magazine featured an article by W.R. Arrasmith. The article's title, "Your Silent Salesman," made the point that "Good terminals make good impressions." Despite years of corporate commitment to the development of a distinctive Greyhound look, Greyhound's most prominent architect offered what should have been long established ideas. The bus terminal he declared was the "first and last impression of bus transportation gained by the traveling public." Arrasmith expressed the rationale behind his design philosophy, and that of Greyhound, noting, "The modern station or rest stop is one of the best silent salesmen the bus industry can have. Much dissatisfaction with bus travel stems from inadequate station and rest stop facilities. The more modern and streamlined the buses become, the sharper and greater this contrast grows."

"Oftentimes travel literature," asserted Arrasmith, "has had a tendency to give the prospective passenger the idea that he or she will be surrounded by comfort, convenience and every facility they could reasonably desire from the time they purchase their ticket until they reach their destination." However, while "bus transportation has grown by leaps and bounds, it will take some time and constant doing to get this 'Young Giant' a complete wardrobe that will stay abreast of his steady and ever increasing growth."

Reflecting the difficulty of labeling the evolving architectural design within modernism is this assertion by Wrenick regarding the St. Paul, Minnesota, terminal. "By 1954 the avant-garde style that appeared immediately after World War II had given way to a more generic modern style. Although elements of the streamline era remained, they were overshadowed by the new style and had become mere tokens of what had formerly been."

Santa Rosa, California. *AACA*

Cleveland, Ohio. *AACA*

GBM

Cleveland, Ohio. *AACA*

GBM

St. Paul, Minnesota. *AACA*

St. Paul, Minnesota. *AACA*

CHAPTER 5

1955-1979: NEW ROADS FOR A NEW ERA

GBM

Five years after publishing Don Eddy's account of a 3,000-mile cross-country trip aboard a Greyhound Silversides Super-Coach, *American Magazine*, January 1955, featured "I Rode the Super-Bus," Evan McLeod Wylie's account of his "2,000-mile scenic cruise from New England to Florida." Wylie offered the reader—and vicarious traveler—a vivid "word-picture" filled with all of the romance of the road Greyhound could have wished for. His account begins with the end of his "2,000-mile bus ride in the latest thing in luxury on rubber tires which had transported me into a new world of safe comfortable travel and vacation adventure." He rhapsodized: "I savored the last bite of broiled pompano, sipped my iced coffee, and ordered a piece of lime pie. A few steps from my breezy restaurant veranda, bathers lolled against a vista of waving palms, white sands, and deep blue waters of the Gulf Stream."

With all of the romance-of-the-road rhetoric possible, Wylie spun his tale. "From the glassed-in observation deck of a fabulous new super-bus, known to its driver as 'The mighty Monster,' I enjoyed a ringside seat at one of the greatest shows on earth—my fellow Americans at work and play amidst the glorious scenery of the Eastern seaboard. I sniffed the tangy salt marshes of Massachusetts, the fragrant piney woods of Virginia, and the scented gardens of old Charleston; wandered through the great groves of moss-bearded live oaks on old plantations, explored ancestral mansions, and sampled my countrymen's favorite dishes, from New England clam chowder to Virginia country ham, Georgia pecan pie, and Florida sea turtle soup. Landmarks of American history from Washington's Mount Vernon to the old Spain of St. Augustine brought me face to face with stirring chapters in 500 years of New World history. A pageant of America—scenic, historic, romantic America—unfolded before me as we rolled down the highways."

Wylie's description of the bus would warm the heart of any Greyhound publicist. "We were riding in a new Greyhound 'Scenicruiser,' a 15-ton, split-level mammoth of a super-bus, the largest and most luxurious vehicle ever seen on the highway." Wylie offered a catalog of important features, including "power steering, power brakes, an electrically controlled, 8-speed, push-button gear shift, [and] a highly efficient air-conditioning system that was changing the air inside the bus every 40 seconds." In particular, "To the right of the stairs was an important innovation in bus travel—a fully equipped washroom with running water, basin, toilet, boudoir mirrors, and other conveniences." The interior design rated raves. Behind the driver "was a 10-passenger forward deck and then a short flight of steps leading to a glassed-in observation deck, where 33 more of us travelers reclined in foam-rubber contour chairs gazing out at the sights through tinted picture windows, overhead skylights, and a panoramic windshield at the front of the top deck."

Reflecting the proclamation of a "New Era in Highway Travel" found in the advertisement featuring Mrs. America, Wylie declared, "Our blue-and-silver behemoth was off on a 1,500 mile dash from New York to Miami. Aside from brief stops for meals and change of drivers, it would roll straight through and reach Florida by the following afternoon, ushering in a new era in highway transportation." Wylie's account of his ride in the new "Super-Bus," Greyhound's Scenicruiser, indicates his romantic adventure did not merely involve a direct ride from New York to Miami. "Our arrival in Baltimore was the signal for me to desert the super-bus for the first of a series of side jaunts and excursions in other busses that were to enrich my southern journey." Wylie's "side jaunts" that included Annapolis, Virginia's Skyline Drive, Washington, D.C., and Mount Vernon offered the kind of romance for travelers Greyhound had long promoted. His prose evokes the sense of adventure prevalent in Greyhound advertising. "The past seemed close at hand on the soft Indian-summer afternoon [...]. History rode with us as we resumed our journey southward."

With the introduction of the Highway Traveler and Scenicruiser, Greyhound, like author Wylie, heralded a "New Era of Travel." Meant to showcase these new buses as material manifestations of Depression- and wartime-era utopian visions, the label also reflected the profound economic, demographic, and cultural changes occurring in America in the 1950s. Characteristics of this "new era" included new buses, new highways, increased income levels sufficient to provide ever-increasing opportunities for discretionary spending, increased leisure time, the availability of affordable consumer goods, new patterns of development, population growth, and an increase in automobile ownership.

The achievement of some of the utopian visions from the 1930s and 1940s, including the new buses, were part of the tremendous output of new consumer goods following World War II. As in the past, the romance of the road—a continuing part of the vision of Greyhound's "new era"—depended upon the interconnectedness of the bus and the road. Greyhound did its part, creating buses featuring the last word in modern style and technology.

"Introducing a great New Era in highway travel!" proclaimed Greyhound's brochure introducing Scenicruiser service. First, Greyhound promised a "New Era in scenic enjoyment!...a brand new conception of American beauty when you travel by Scenicruiser." With prose in the best romance-of-the-road-tradition the brochure explained, "Meet the real America by Scenicruiser! If you had traveled this Land before—but never really experienced the sightseeing adventure and drama found only along America's great highways...then you're ready for a Scenicruiser trip. You'll thrill to the broad sweep of beauty in the rolling countryside, magnificent mountain peaks reaching to touch cotton-white clouds, the great forests, sparkling lakes, flashing streams." Greyhound also promised a "New Era in travel history! Once in many years, there is a vital change in transportation—one that completely revises all previous standards of travel ease, comfort, luxury. Such a new era in travel begins now, with the Greyhound Scenicruiser, most remarkable motor vehicle of the last half century...it represents an entirely new conception of relaxed and effortless travel, sightseeing pleasure without parallel."

The government also played its part, creating an entirely new standard for roads with the passage of the Federal Highway Act of 1956, signed into law on June 29th by President Dwight D. Eisenhower. As the interstate system developed, the nature of travel changed significantly. The limited access interstate highway, seeking a new route as often as possible, became a means to an end, a line connecting distant places with little regard for points in between. Discussed previously, Drake Hokanson, in *The Lincoln Highway: Main Street Across America,* contends the interstates "changed the way Americans traveled, and changed the way they looked at the land." America became a landscape conquered by technology. Critical of the interstate highway system, this perspective offers a nostalgic look at the way travel used to be as a kind of touchstone for the way it ought to be today. Hokanson defines travel in terms of a wistful longing for a golden age in some mythical past. Such ages seldom exist. The fact that Greyhound promoted the romance of the road does not guarantee that travelers actually experienced it, but it seems clear that Greyhound experienced significant success persuading the traveling public of its reality.

In part, due to unintended and unanticipated consequences, the interstates altered the landscape for the romance of the road. Whether representative of other situations or truly unique, an example may offer insight into the larger story. As originally planned, Interstate 35 north from Minneapolis and St. Paul, Minnesota, featured an exit/entrance at Wyoming, Minnesota, with a population of approximately 500. There were no exits planned for access to the larger community of Forest Lake—population approximately 2,000—only three miles to the south. Efforts by Forest Lake officials subsequently resulted in the construction of additional exits/entrances. That this occurred suggests those responsible for the initial planning of the interstate system did not always understand the impact nor anticipate the growth and development spawned by the freeway especially at entrance/exit points. A corollary of the interstate is the national standardization of taste and culture with the ubiquitous fast food restaurant franchise, a staple of the interstate roadside. Interstate 25 by-passed Corbin, Kentucky, site of Colonel (an honorific title bestowed by Kentucky's governor) Harlan Sanders' original restaurant. Sanders far-sighted response was to follow the new highway and create Kentucky Fried Chicken franchises along the interstates.

The interstate system has significantly shaped the way Americans travel. To some extent, the loss of contact with aspects of America's history and culture is another unintended consequence of developing the destination as the ultimate end and all else, the means. These trips to a final destination do not include side trips or visits along the way to many of the places, people, or things that interested past travelers. Actually, travel in the past took people to the same major destinations—Yellowstone, the Grand Canyon, Niagara Falls—but the trip to them allowed the traveler to take in more; to be part of a richer, more complex tableau of travel.

With 12-foot wide lanes, no traffic signals, or intersections, the interstate system promised the kind of highway perfectly suited to the Highway Traveler and the Scenicruiser. But these new highways also suited the automobile traveler. The continued growth of the automobile should not have come as a surprise—it was a phenomenon that began in the 1920s. As a reminder, the railroads had long ago learned the automobile had the greatest impact on railroad passenger levels. The automobile increasingly impacted travel by bus. The interstates contributed to the belief in the necessity for speed, a criterion easily met by the airplane. Additionally, these highways seemed to offer support for promoting Greyhound's long-standing goal of the democratization of travel. Years later, Norman Mineta, Transportation Secretary reflected this belief. "In other parts of the world, they are envious of our highway system, not only because it is an economic force, but it has become a democratizing force as well."

Author Michael S. Sweeney asserts the nature of the interstates "nurtured confidence but little romance. Before the interstates appeared, songwriters penned odes to the highway. Bobby Troup wrote '(Get Your Kicks On) Route 66' while traveling along the celebrated old road to the California coast. The pop-rock group America sang about 'Ventura Highway,' and Bob Dylan immortalized Minnesota's 'Highway 61.' But the sameness of the Interstate Highway System, where one interchange looked pretty much like another, inspired few poets."

Clearly, the "new era of travel" announced by Greyhound took place in a "new" America. While continuing to pursue utopian visions, the ominous mushroom cloud of nuclear Armageddon, tempered American's optimism. Historians periodize historical time—in some ways no different than Greyhound's advertising writers labeling the time as the "new era of travel." For the historian, it was the "Cold War era." Both efforts seek to define an age with a label to attach characteristics and thus meaning. Advertisers create labels to define an era as it is occurring—a way to sell or promote something. Historians usually create labels after the fact, but it too is an effort to persuade others that the label is an accurate reflection of reality. Applying two labels to a time period suggests each offers a way to see a facet of the world, none complete in itself.

For our analysis, a "new era of travel" is most relevant. The 1950s witnessed a kind of "perfect storm" of factors with the development of the interstate highway system the final piece of the jigsaw puzzle that profoundly altered America and moved the nation in new directions. The increasing income levels with fringe benefits that included paid vacations and the availability of increased leisure time offered the opportunity to travel more for leisure. The automobile became a key symbol of prosperity and individual success—the make a clue to the level. The automobile also allowed the individual and the "baby boom" families created following the war to travel and find the romance of the road in their own car. While not new developments, increasing income levels with greater amounts for discretionary use and increased leisure time—phenomenon that, like the growth of automobile ownership, began in the 1920s—significantly shaped the culture.

Changes also included new patterns of settlement and development. The suburbs, while not new, became the site of major growth. The returning GIs, who came home with dreams to fulfill, bought homes with GI and FHA financing in new suburban subdivisions. This decentralization required the means to travel back and forth to work. The template for future commercial development became Southdale, located in Edina, Minnesota. Completed in 1956, it was the first enclosed shopping mall in the United States. Both depended upon widespread automobile ownership. Initially a suburban necessity, the automobile became a means for discretionary travel. Although new attractions tantalized and beckoned the traveler, travel destinations continued to offer the romance of the road, but the means to get there now had another viable option.

Greyhound faced increased competition from this viable option, the family vacation taken in the family automobile. In *Are We There Yet? The Golden Age of American Family Vacations*, historian Susan Sessions Rugh presents a cultural history of this particular kind of American family vacation from the end of World War II until the 1970s. Much of her analysis recognizes the postwar developments that also impacted Greyhound. According to Rugh, based on the ideal of family togetherness, the family vacation became a "ritual for the sake of the family." Specifically, "Americans justified taking a family vacation out of their commitment to the idea that travel provided a way to educate children as citizens."

Automobile manufacturers promoted the family vacation. A necessity in the increasingly suburbanized postwar world, the automobile could also become literally a vehicle for family togetherness. Rugh argues the automobile became a "home on wheels, an extension of the domestic space, and thus represented a sense of security for the traveling family on the road." In particular, it became "a cocoon that buffered the family from the outside world and increased their sense of security while they traveled to unfamiliar places." However, as most parents remember, family togetherness often degenerates into family squabbles as territorial disputes involving the rear seat erupt between siblings.

Greyhound advertising acknowledged the increasing popularity of the automobile while asserting the bus would be less expensive, more comfortable, and more relaxing—after all, someone else did the driving. This 1955 folder, depicting a "typical" family, and thus symbolizing all families, addressed problematic aspects of the family vacation taken in the family automobile. "Wherever you go by Greyhound you'll discover America's beauty close-up all along the way. You'll relax in the deep-cushioned adjustable chairs, sightseeing or napping in the luxury of controlled temperature and ventilation. Congenial fellow passengers—dependable, friendly drivers help make the trip even more enjoyable. Stopovers are easily arranged." Continuing to promote Amazing America Tours, Greyhound offered complete vacation planning services. Traveling by bus, Greyhound suggested, would be more likely to provide the traveler with the opportunity to experience the romance of the road. **[fig. 213]**

Rugh asserts that the family vacation involved "searching for an affirmative national history better labeled as *heritage*. In the wake of World War II, Americans traveled to historic sites and museums. "We can label these travels *pilgrimages* because the destination is a special place, a place that has become set apart or 'sacred.'" In the process, "Traveling together as a family in a ritual of civic pilgrimage,

Fig. 213. *MBS*

parents and children reinforced their sense of what it meant to be an American." In fact, "making the journey is evidence of their strong belief in the value of the travel ritual." Bus travel negates none of these opportunities. Families can participate in pilgrimages and visit the same sacred places by bus as much as by automobile.

Families traveling by automobile on the interstate highways preferred motels over hotels. Less expensive than hotels and just off the highway, motels offered parking close to the room and no tips for service. The motel also offered amenities that people did not have at home—color TV and a pool. Since the interstates by-passed many cities and towns a shift in commercial development catering to the traveler wishing to avoid a trip into town ensued. Greyhound terminals, centrally located in cities, became less desirable, except as final destinations. This development may have influenced the decision to create Greyhound Rent-A-Car operations in these terminals—rent a car and take a side trip.

Perhaps most significantly and ultimately, the reason families traveled by automobile is that such a "family vacation" offers autonomy for the individual at a level that is impossible for families traveling together on a bus or for that matter, any form of public transportation. Greyhound promoted tailoring travel with stopovers and side trips at the discretion of each traveler. Writers taking their vacation by bus mention these enriching experiences. Traveling in the family car, however, meant the freedom to make changes at will; to vary the route; to stop as needed for gas, to take restroom breaks, and to take in unanticipated sights and attractions. In addition, the cost per person would generally be less than the cost for the entire family to take the bus.

Within this context of increasing competition from the automobile, the leadership of Greyhound changed in 1956. Arthur S. Genet became Greyhound's president, replacing the departed Orville Caesar, president since 1946. Suggesting Genet represented the new leader for Greyhound's "new era of travel," *Business Week*, March 16, 1957, assessed his leadership and the changes he implemented at Greyhound. The article indicated Genet's "assignment was clear: to reverse the decline of Greyhound from a 1953 peak." Genet, who declared, "bus vacations will be the nation's most popular form of diversion," spent the first six weeks of his presidency traveling in a Scenicruiser equipped with a "handsome executive office" investigating Greyhound operations and facilities.

One of Genet's actions resulted in a "purge" (or firing) of 259 "supervisors below the level of president." Genet declared, "They didn't have what it takes, to start with. Getting our house in order should have taken place 10 to 15 years ago." Interesting, since this would place the date for this as early as 1941, the eve of World War II, and during the era of the original Greyhound founders, or in 1946, the year Orville Caesar assumed the presidency. Genet established Greyhound Rent-A-Car, Inc. Inaugurated in Cleveland, the initial success of the rental car business led Genet to mandate the expansion of the service to 122 terminals in 12 months.

The article also linked Greyhound's future success with the new interstate system. Noting the declining railroad passenger business and the effort Greyhound would make to gain from this, Genet added, "And if another factor is needed, we certainly have it in the coast-to-coast highway construction program." *Business Week* echoed Genet. "Meanwhile, the turnpikes are giving Greyhound a new 'super' right of way that permits buses to compete with the railroads for long-distance passengers."

Genet's leadership in the "New Era" proved short-lived. Some analysts suggest the expense of implementing the rental car program too quickly, along with an accompanying lack of oversight, were key factors leading to Genet's replacement by Fred Ackerman in 1958, after only two years. *Forbes* Magazine, May 1, 1963, also reviewed Arthur Genet's efforts to diversify into the rental car business, calling it a "costly flop." The article added other reasons for his dismissal. "Genet borrowed so freely that by the start of 1958 long-term debt had reached a worrisome 35% of the total capital in the business" with losses that totaled $6 million.

To promote the desirability of long-distance travel on the interstates as well as connecting highways, Greyhound modernized and upgraded its long established Post House Restaurants. A more detailed look at the whole range of Greyhound's food service activities indicates the company's response to the changing American roadside. Venturing outside the Post House format, Greyhound added restaurants in Holiday Inn motels in 1957. From a high of 141 Post Houses in 1956, the number gradually decreased to "nearly 120" by 1966. In that year Greyhound opened three "I-Highway" restaurants featuring distinctive red roofs and "located along the Federal Interstate Highway System." The Post House restaurants, located along long-established routes, provided food service at locations unlikely to offer the level of service to meet Greyhound's standards. The new routes established by the interstates bypassed many of these locations. In late 1963, Greyhound acquired Horne's Enterprises, Inc. that featured "roadside stores" with "eye-catching" yellow roofs, providing "one-stop-service for the traveler: tasty food economically priced, gift merchandise, lodging and gasoline for cars." These reflect the ubiquitous convenience stores that dot the current landscape.

While president, Genet refocused Greyhound's advertising starting with retaining a new advertising agency. For 1957, Greyhound devoted less to print media with 54% of its $5 million budget going for TV and radio advertising. (Greyhound first advertised on television in 1951.) *Business Week* noted, "For 13 weeks Greyhound will have one-third of the commercial time on the Steve Allen Sunday night hour on NBC-TV. The sound track includes a jingle—'It's a comfort to ride the bus—and leave the driving to us'—in the best singing commercial vein." The article also acknowledged the impact of the increasing popularity of the automobile and the family vacation by automobile. "The entire advertising campaign will be slanted to attract the private automobile driver to Greyhound buses for his intercity travel."

Greyhound's promotional efforts also included a memorable campaign to highlight its iconic "Living Symbol." Greyhound's 1958 *Annual Report* explained: "Two years ago a spindle-legged Greyhound puppy left Clay Center, Kansas, for the television stages of New York. Then one night she stepped before the cameras and into millions of American homes—and hearts. And that is how the world's most famous symbol came to life. This living Greyhound—called Steverino then—grew and grew, was seen by more and more people and soon became famous." Shown in a 1957 photograph with Steve Allen, also called Steverino (On Allen's show comedian Louis Nye greeted Allen with "Hi Ho, Steverino."), she became Lady Greyhound in 1958. **[fig. 214]** She was crowned Queen of National Dog Week, turned into an "honorary cat" to reign as Queen of National Cat Week, helped celebrate the 48th birthday of the Camp Fire girls, helped promote the March of Dimes and Easter Seals, and became Dog of the Year in 1960. In 1962, Lady Greyhound participated in the festivities associated with the world premiere of the motion picture, 'The Music Man," at Mason City, Iowa. Lady Greyhound rode at the head of the parade in a Buick Roadmaster convertible. The *Annual Report*

Fig. 214. Steve Allen and Lady Greyhound, 1957. *GBM*

also noted fifty busloads of bands from all over the United States that performed at the premiere utilized Greyhound—"paying customers all."

The civil rights struggles of the 1960s involved Greyhound. *The Philadelphia Inquirer,* May 12, 2001, covered the 40th anniversary of the Freedom Riders. Primarily college students, the Freedom Riders, groups of black and white civil rights activists, traveled on public buses including Greyhounds in May 1961 to protest long established racial segregation and discrimination practices involving buses and bus facilities in the South. "At segregated bus stations, black riders tried to use white waiting rooms and bathrooms, while whites tried to use facilities set aside for blacks. When the riders were beaten and arrested along the way, hundreds more joined the campaign. Eventually more than 1,000 people took part." Hank Thomas, a 19-year old college student in 1961, "was aboard a Greyhound bus outside Anniston, Ala., when it was attacked and firebombed by a mob of segregationists. Smoke filled the bus, he said, and some members of the mob outside held the doors closed until the exploding gas tank scared them away. Thomas and the others on the bus escaped, but about 350 people were arrested for violating state segregation laws." The article noted efforts to create a Freedom Riders Museum in the former Greyhound Terminal in Selma, Alabama, the scene of beatings of Freedom Riders.

Also in 1961, Greyhound established Greyhound at the World's Fair, Inc. "to handle" the company's participation in the 1964-1965 New York World's Fair. According to Greyhound's 1961 *Annual Report,* "Greyhound will provide all internal transportation, conduct guided tours in several languages and will man the information booths on the Fair grounds." The *Annual Report* recalled Greyhound's role in providing the transportation for Chicago's A Century of Progress in 1933-1934 and the 1939-1940 New York World's Fair, and noted, "In addition, Greyhound will have its own building at the Fair. **[fig. 215]** This structure will house ticket counters, travel and tour information booths, package express facilities, and specially-designed exhibits on buses, other corporate services and scenic attractions throughout the U.S.A. Also planned are a 1,500-seat theater to show Fair visitors Greyhound films and a fully-automatic vending restaurant which can serve 20 meals a minute and will be operated by Greyhound Post Houses." In addition, Greyhound provided food service for the Rheingold Beer restaurant featuring a "tavern, sidewalk café, town house, food kiosks and strolling vendors" located in a "quaint park-like setting reminiscent of New York at the turn of the century." This is a 1963 artist's depiction of Greyhound's planned exhibit and restaurant building.

"Welcome to the Fair of the Century!" declared Greyhound publicity. "As you enter through any of the eight main gates, you'll find yourself in the fascinating World of the Future." Continuing the tradition established by past exhibitions and fairs, the 1964-1965 New York World's Fair offered utopian visions and optimistic dreams about the future. Regarded by promoters as the "greatest attraction of the century," the Fair occupied Flushing Meadows, the same site as the Fair in 1939 and 1940. It featured over 140 pavilions and exhibits from seventeen individual states and the combined New England States and "countries all over the world" including Greece, India, Argentina, Ireland, Sierra Leone, Jordan, Thailand, Japan, and the United States. Organizations such as Billy Graham, the Boy Scouts, the Mormon Church, and the Russian Orthodox Church also sponsored exhibits.

Fig. 215. New York World's Fair. *AACA*

The "Leading firms throughout the United States" that exhibited included American Express, Chun King, DuPont, IBM, Ford, General Motors, Chrysler, RCA, and Schaefer Brewing. United States Steel constructed the fair's symbol, the Unisphere, a giant skeletal globe of the world.

As with the 1933-1934 Century of Progress and the 1939-1940 New York World's Fair, Greyhound provided a "new-as-tomorrow fleet" of unique vehicles for transportation within the 646-acre site. The "futuristic Escorter lounge car," designed for up to four passengers and manufactured by the Kalamazoo Manufacturing Company, represented a marked departure from past fair and exhibition vehicles. **[fig. 216]** This color image provides an airbrushed view of a prototype Escorter while the black and white photograph provides a look at an actual production version. **[fig. 217]** In its World's Fair brochure Greyhound noted, "The promenades and roadways alone are nearly forty miles long!"—reason enough for "going the Greyhound way."

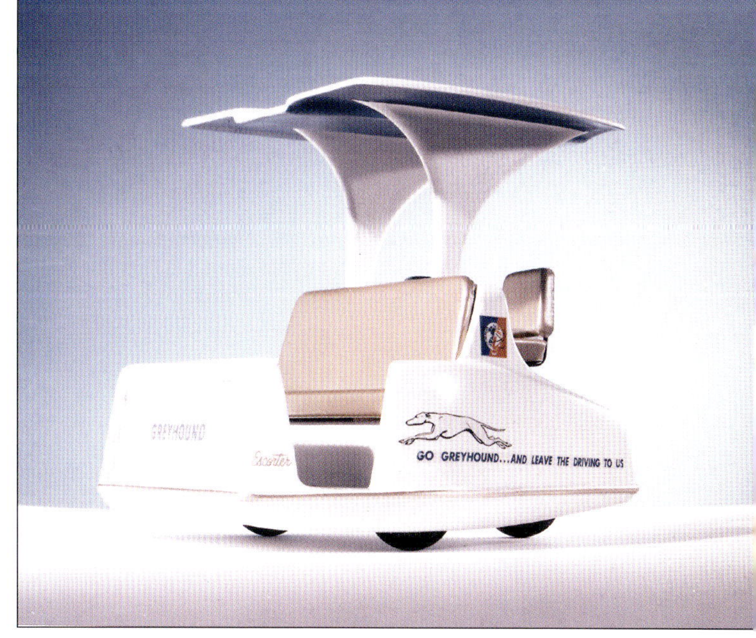

Fig. 216. Greyhound Escorter prototype. *AACA*

In 1963, continuing a long-established practice, Greyhound officials conducted a christening ceremony in Chicago for the "Ultra-modern Glide-a-Ride." The "futuristic tractor train" designed to "provide special service to World's Fair patrons" fol-

Fig. 217. Greyhound Escorter. *AACA*

lowed the concept of the "sidewalk crawlers" based on an International truck used at the 1939-1940 New York World's Fair. Clark Equipment Company, Battle Creek, Michigan, manufactured these vehicles. Reflecting the modernistic design aesthetic of the early 1960s, the 60-passenger Glide-a-Ride and the Escorter are right at home with a glass and steel curtain wall International style office tower in the background. **[fig. 218]** Fairgoers rode the Glide-a-Ride for 25 cents each time they boarded at one of the more than two dozen stations throughout the Fair grounds. Greyhound provided over 300 vehicles for use at the Fair.

On location at the Fair, four passengers pose in the Greyhound Escorter; among them at the far right is noted radio and television celebrity Arthur Godfrey. To provide the needed visibility, the driver-guide occupies a position on an elevated seat at the rear. **[fig. 219]** "The Escorter lounge-car offers luxurious, personalized service to the entire Fair, including roadways and walkways not available to other vehicles. Pick your own route...choose a pre-planned tour... or engage the Escorter on a meter basis. Rates are $9.00 per hour for two passengers with a surcharge of $1.00 for each third and fourth passengers. Minimum fare: $3.00."

In addition to the Escorter and Glide-a-Ride vehicles, Greyhound also provided Scenicruiser buses for sightseeing. According to Greyhound publicity, these vehicles served Fair visitors from "more than 30

Fig. 218. Greyhound Glide-a-Ride. *AACA*

Fig. 219. Greyhound Escorter at work. *AACA*

stations operated on the five route-miles of highway encircling the fairgrounds, and on routes from the parking lots to the main admission gates, as well as throughout the grounds." A $3.00 "Grand Sightseeing Deluxe lectured tour that covers the entire Fair" was available and lasted for about an hour and a half. Greyhound at the World's Fair, Inc. provided information booths to provide transportation and sightseeing information for Fair visitors. Greyhound noted, "Many of the employees will be proficient in foreign languages and will conduct guided tours." Greyhound Fair personnel totaled approximately 1,500.

Greyhound's bus fleet had seen no significant change since the introductions of the Highway Traveler and the Scenicruiser in 1953 and 1954 respectively. These buses had ushered in Greyhound's "new era" of travel. In 1960, Greyhound ordered a new version of the Highway Traveler, with that label dropped in favor of Scenicruiser Service added to the body. Produced by General Motors, the new 38-passenger single-level buses, featured a restroom, air conditioning, "panoramic windows" air suspension ride, and "adjustable, reclining seats for maximum travel com-

Fig. 220. First diesel-powered Greyhound, 1960. *AACA*

Fig. 221. Last of the General Motors buses. *GBM*

Fig. 222. MCI-built Greyhound. *AACA*

fort." V-8 diesel engines powered the buses "for the first time in company history," exclaimed Greyhound's publicity. **[fig. 220]** Greyhound ordered these models with three different paint schemes through 1964, while refurbishing the dual-level Scenicruisers and identifying them as a Super Scenicriuser.

After a very long association, dating from the 1930s, Greyhound ordered its final General Motors bus with delivery during 1966 and 1967. **[fig. 221]** The impetus for this significant departure from tradition was Greyhound's decision to manufacture its own buses. This involved Motor Coach Industries, Inc. (MCI, Inc.), an American subsidiary of Greyhound Corporation, established in 1962, and located in a newly constructed plant at Pembina, North Dakota, and the already existing Motor Coach Industries Limited, Manitoba, Canada, a subsidiary of Greyhound Lines of Canada. MCI Ltd. manufactured buses for Greyhound's Canadian operation and sold buses to other Canadian bus lines. Limited production of buses by this combined operation began in mid-1963. Greyhound also intended to continue to sell part of the production to other bus operators. Earlier, Greyhound's 1962 *Annual Report* provided an explanation for shareholders. "Bus shells [for the MC-5 Challenger and of course, future buses] will be manufactured and painted, and interiors finished by Motor Coach Industries Limited. The completed shells will be shipped from Winnipeg to Pembina—65 miles—where Motor Coach Industries, Inc., the United States bus-building company, will assemble the buses." The *Annual Report* indicated an expected production rate of 200 buses per year by the end of 1963. **[fig. 222]**

In 1967, more than a decade since introducing something significantly different to the public, Greyhound announced the "road testing of the first dramatically new bus since the mid-1950s." This "experimental model, the MC-6X, was tested on express runs between Chicago and New York City. The new bus—50 of which will be delivered in 1968—is five feet longer and more than a foot higher and six inches wider than the current single-level bus. Powered by a 12-cylinder GM engine, it was developed over the last four years by Motor Coach Industries." The bus featured a cargo capacity twice the size of the existing single level buses in Greyhound's fleet, a benefit for growth in Greyhound's Package Express delivery service. Greyhound road tested the MC-6X in California, Arizona, and Nevada as well as between Chicago and New York City in 1968. A second prototype sent to Europe early in 1968 for installation of a new diesel engine developed by Mercedes-Benz returned to the United States for road testing. **[fig. 223]**

Motor Coach Industries, Inc. also introduced the MC-7 Scenicruiser in 1968. **[fig. 224]** *Road and Track* magazine, in a marked departure, road tested the bus for its April 1969 issue. "Having reached the indeterminate age of over-40," author Tony Hogg declared, "I find that one of the things I most enjoy on a long trip is not driving." Hogg noted the key differences between the MC-6 Supercruiser and the MC-7. "The MC-6 is bigger overall; and because it is 102 in. wide it is not at present legal, although Greyhound has a permit to run its two prototypes between New York and Chicago. The MC-7 is legal, and some 50 are in regular use." While both models measured

Fig. 223. Supercruiser, 1968. *AACA*

40 feet long, the MC-7 measured "a conventional 96 inches wide." A General Motors V-8 diesel powered the MC-7, while the MC-6 featured a V-12. "From the styling viewpoint, the new models are superb examples of good industrial design. However," Hogg asserted, "they do not quite reach the standard set by the old Greyhound Scenicruiser, which came off Raymond Loewy's drawing board many years ago and is surely one of the most handsome vehicles on the road today."

Hogg's verdict for the MC-7 would cheer Greyhound officials. "Summing up Greyhound's MC-7 is quite easy; it appears to be a magnificent piece of machinery." However, his evaluation of Greyhound facilities would not provide any cheer. "If Greyhound wants to attract more customers, I suspect the first move should be to update some of its terminals. [M]ost terminals leave something to be desired and some are downright scruffy."

The condition of the terminals noted in Hogg's 1969 *Road and Track* article offers a commentary on Greyhound corporate policies. In 1961, according to Greyhound public relations information, it established a diversification policy that by 1969 resulted in the establishment of subsidiaries in the fields of food, finance, and service. By the end of 1968, nearly 38 percent of Greyhound's profits came from outside the bus business compared to 5 percent in 1961.

Fig. 224. MC-7 Senicruiser, 1968. *AACA*

The 1969 *Annual Report* offered this definition: "The Greyhound Corporation is a multi-industry company with more than 100 active subsidiaries." Back in its May 1, 1963 issue, *Forbes* magazine reported that Greyhound had "The nicest kind of problem. Greyhound's bus business is piling up profits at a record-making clip. A major diversification move is working out splendidly. But success is creating a new problem: what to do with growing amounts of spare cash." Greyhound management decided increased diversification was the answer to this problem. *Annual Reports* over the years covered the growing

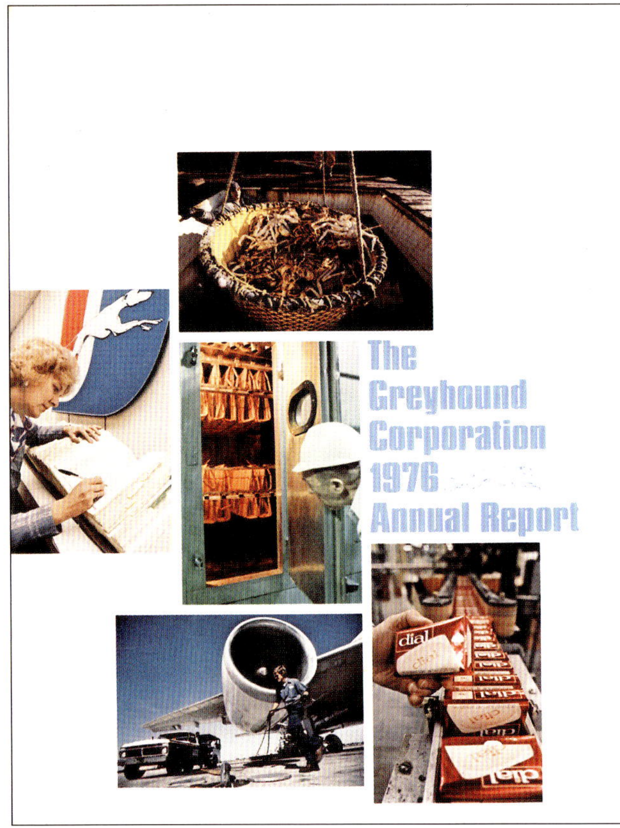

Fig. 225. *MBS*

Fig. 226. 1971 Super-7. *GBM*

Fig. 227. Super-7 Turbocruiser. *AACA*

number of acquisitions. In 1973, for example, Greyhound acquired the "Burn Treatment Skin Bank," while the 1974 edition dealt with the disappointing losses of the "Greyhound cattle feeding operation" and the "Armour poultry operation." Greyhound's goal of diversification influenced the allocation of the corporation's resources. For example, in 1969, when Tony Hogg criticized the conditions in Greyhound terminals, the company allocated resources to acquire Armour and Company, producers of meat products and Dial soap and deodorant. The 1976 *Annual Report* cover reflects the "multi-industry" nature of acquisition-minded Greyhound. **[fig. 225]**

By 1971, Motor Coach Industries had become the "largest producer of intercity buses in North America. Modifications to the MC-7 Scenicruiser resulted in a Super 7 designation. **[fig. 226]** As with many other vehicle manufacturers including General Motors, Ford, Chrysler, Autocar, and Freightliner, Greyhound invested in turbine engine development. In 1972, Greyhound placed four MCI-7 Super 7 Turbocruiser buses in regular service. **[fig. 227]** Also in 1972, four years prior to the celebration, Greyhound introduced "Bi-centennial-inspired" red, white, and blue paint schemes. Henceforth, all Greyhound buses featured these colors.

Motor Coach Industries introduced the "revolutionary" MC-8 Americruiser in 1973. **[fig. 228]** The Greyhound fleet of over 5,000 buses would eventually include nearly 2,000 43-passenger Americruisers. Subsequently, Greyhound developed the gas-turbine-powered MC-8 Turbocruiser. As the signage on the bus indicates, the U.S. Department of Energy sponsored this demonstration program. Curtailed funding and the inherent limitations of gas-turbine engines for buses led to the termination of this development effort. **[fig. 229]**

In late 1978, Greyhound introduced the MC-9, the fifth model developed since the establishment of Motor Coach Industries in 1962, adding it to its fleet starting in 1979. The interior view illustrates the impact of the design's large windows. **[fig. 230, 231]**

Initially proclaimed by Greyhound in 1954, the "new era of travel" had promised a bright future. The Federal Interstate Highway system and Greyhound's

Fig. 228. 1973 MC-8 Americruiser. *AACA*

new buses with innovative features seemed to be the combination needed for significant growth of intercity motor coach travel. However, automobile manufacturers and eager consumers also responded to the construction of the interstate highway. The era witnessed the introduction of new automobiles designed for comfortable "turnpike cruising" and a tremendous increase in automobile ownership. The choice increasingly made by consumers was to travel by automobile and the American roadside changed to respond to this phenomenon. Greyhound ridership totals reflect this change. In 1960, Greyhound transported 100,000,000 passengers, a level never again achieved. By 1979, ridership totaled 55 million. More significant changes lay on the road ahead. For Greyhound, the road would be anything but romantic.

Fig. 230. 1978 MC-9. *AACA*

Fig. 229. MC-8 Turbocruiser. *AACA*

Fig. 231. MC-9 interior. *AACA*

Greyhound Terminal Album: 1955-1979

Greyhound terminal architecture now reflected the increasingly popular International Style variant of modern architecture. While intended to demonstrate Greyhound's embrace of the newest design expressions, these non-descript terminals lacked a distinctive "Greyhound look" in contrast with earlier terminal designs. Determining the occupant of these structures would be difficult without the Greyhound signage. Also problematic is the extent to which travelers would consider them "portals to pleasure" compared to earlier Greyhound terminals.

San Bernardino, California. *AACA*

San Jose, California. *AACA*

Milwaukee, Wisconsin. *GBM*

Tacoma, Washington. *AACA*

Santa Cruz, California. *AACA*

Vallejo, California. *AACA*

Bakersfield, California. *AACA*

CHAPTER 6

THE LESS-ROMANTIC ROAD: SINCE 1980

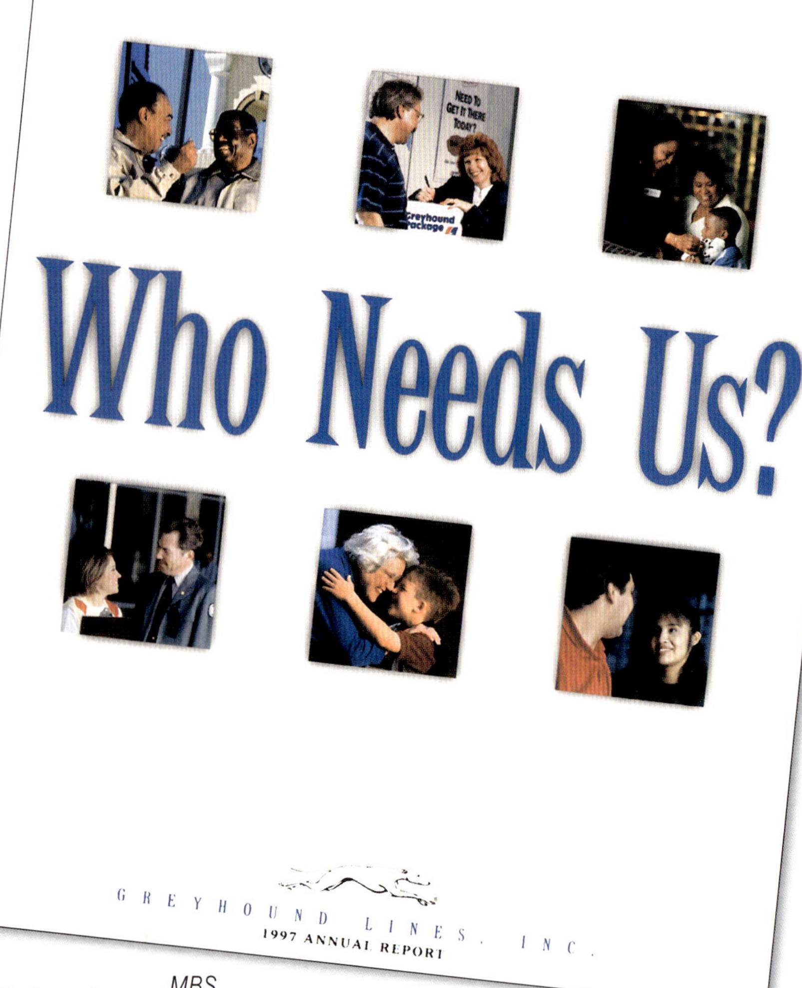

MBS

The 1983 film, *National Lampoon's Vacation*, offers the opportunity to see that the drama of the family vacation described in *Are We There Yet?,* as a quest for romance in the old sense of adventure was no longer possible. To the refrain of "Holiday Road," the utopian dream of the romantic automobile-based family vacation becomes a dystopian nightmare as Clark and the rest of the Griswold family—Ellen, Rusty, and Audrey—encounter one disaster after another. The adventure, salvaged in the end by a visit to Walley World, a dream world destination, is part of a much larger drama featuring the still prominent but increasingly problematic quest for travel that embodies the romance of the road.

The station wagon, the golden chariot of the family vacation, is the Wagon Queen Family Truckster, a bad dream come to life; served up by the delightfully smarmy salesman, Ed, as the ultimate vehicle for "takin' the whole tribe 'cross country." Foreshadowing the entire adventure, Ed offers these reassuring words about the Metallic Pea with wood appliqué Family Truckster to Clark: "If you think you hate it now…wait 'till you drive it."

Clark, full of a mixture of civic pride, patriotism, chamber of commerce boosterism, and naiveté offers a narrative of romance as the trip unfolds, spinning tales of lore and legend about this great nation to an ever-increasingly unappreciative audience. Besides the "Mighty Mississip'," who could resist the "House of Mud," or the "Second largest ball of twine only four short hours away?" Romance as adventure, however, becomes misadventure, thrills and excitement part of a variety of disasters. As the family threatens mutiny and wants to fly home, Clark takes a stand. "This is no longer a vacation, it's a quest, a quest for fun."

Along the way, Clark encounters a beautiful woman and her Ferrari, symbols of the unattainable romance of the road, the rabbit that always eludes the greyhound. Despite the disasters, the family arrives at the promised land of fun, Walley World, only to find it has closed for two weeks. While holding the security guard hostage, a gun wielding Clark admits the family had "spent two weeks of living hell driving out here." Roy Walley, the redeemer, saves the vacation refusing to press charges and everyone rides off into the sunset on the roller coaster.

Describing the Clark Griswold he portrayed, Chevy Chase declared, "Clark has the romantic ideal of what the great American family vacation should be. His heart is in the right place, it's just that everything that can go wrong does go wrong."

In many ways the story of the Griswold family vacation mirrors the fading dreams of the romance of the road for Greyhound. Ridership declined throughout the 1980s and 1990s. In 1980, Greyhound ridership totaled 54 million, falling to 33 million in 1985, with a low of 15 million passengers in 1993. While ridership increased to 26 million by 1999, it still represented less that half the ridership of Greyhound in 1980.

As it struggled to remain financially viable, Greyhound also vainly struggled to create a meaningful identity. While efforts by management often referred to the "road" and acknowledged history and tradition, the bottom line of fares and revenue became the defining element. Such an identity offered little in the way of the excitement and adventure promoted in the past. Historically, Greyhound's successful efforts to democratize travel, to make it affordable, convenient, and comfortable for the masses, had materialized within the context of marketing efforts to promote the romance of the road.

Greyhound's 1983 *Annual Report*, noting the $8.8 million loss for the Transportation Group offered this explanation: "Obviously, group performance was negatively affected by the 47-day strike at Greyhound Lines which effectively wiped out any chance for a profitable year, and which seriously eroded the profitability of our other transportation companies which interline with Greyhound Lines." The *Report* also noted the 1982 fare wars caused by a wage freeze granted "to one of our largest competitors who then took the concessions and channeled them into a massive effort to undercut fares. We chose to meet the fares, even though our 30% to 50% higher labor costs culminated in a $16 million operating loss at Greyhound Lines."

In the 1930s, bus companies competed with each other by lowering rates often below the level of profitability. Greyhound favored government regulation to reduce the impact of the hundreds of small bus lines offering low fares. However, throughout the 1970s, Greyhound urged the deregulation of the transportation industry. In a "be careful what you wish for" scenario, the 1983 *Annual Report* declared the "new deregulated transportation environment had presented Greyhound Lines with a maze of blind alleys and dead ends." In addition to the bus fare war "airline deregulation had spawned dozens of new, feisty airlines whose bare bones operating policies and non-union workforce allowed them not only to challenge the established airlines in this country, but bus operators as well, offering fares that were as low as half those of intercity bus lines."

Within the context of a deregulated industry in general and a 47-day strike in particular, Greyhound offered a measured response. "And yet, precisely because of the strike, Greyhound Lines is now on the road back. This does not imply a return to the 'good old days' of bus travel nor an attempt to roll back time." The 1983 *Annual Report* also noted, "For those of us who share a real affection for Greyhound Lines, and its rich history and traditions, 'the road back' has the potential to become the road forward." The import of this assessment is the acknowledgement that despite affection for history and tradition, the past would not be a guide to the future. The "good old days" of Greyhound's past would not be the "road back" to success.

In 1954 Greyhound had declared a "new era of travel." However, by 1986, John W. Teets, Greyhound Corporation Chairman, declared, "This is the end of an era." One of many newspapers, the *Oakland* [California] *Press*, December 24, 1986, carried the Associated Press story of the "end of the era." The "Greyhound Corp., parent of the nation's largest intercity bus line, said it would sell the subsidiary to a Dallas investor group for more than $350 million." The article continued, noting, "The company's announcement comes amid declining ridership and its failure to reach a mutually acceptable agreement with bus drivers and other employees for a new contract. Rank and file union members had rejected a tentative contract agreement reached in October. Ridership has dropped steadily in recent years because of competition from low-cost airlines." The Greyhound Corporation subsequently changed its name to the Dial Corporation.

Nearly six months later, on June 20, 1987, the *Oakland Press* covered the Greyhound Lines Inc. announcement of "the agreement to buy Trailways

Corp. for $80 million in a deal," noting that, "if approved by the government, this would make it the country's only national intercity bus company." Fred Currey, Greyhound Chairman and former head of Trailways (1975-1979), had led the "Dallas investor group" that purchased Greyhound and now declared, "Without intervention, the collapse of Trailways is imminent." Unanswered is why Greyhound should intervene and spend $80 million to prevent a Trailways collapse.

In March 1990, substantially all of the bus drivers, clerical workers and mechanics represented by the Amalgamated Transit Union went on strike. Greyhound continued operations by hiring replacement drivers and most striking workers, other than drivers, returned to work. This situation, however, led to violence against Greyhound's buses and facilities. The revenue losses and expenses associated with the strike exhausted Greyhound's cash resources, and in June 1990 it filed a voluntary petition under Chapter 11 of the United States Bankruptcy Code, emerging from bankruptcy in October 1991. During reorganization, Greyhound sold "certain assets of Eagle, its bus manufacturing subsidiary" in October 1991. Eagle Manufacturing, Brownsville, Texas, acquired as part of Greyhound's purchase of Trailways, manufactured buses for Trailways. An example is this 1988 Eagle Model 15. **[fig. 232]** In the last quarter of 1990, Greyhound had "shut down Eagle," releasing all production employees. Greyhound eliminated all Eagle buses from its fleet by the end of October 1991.

In the 1994 *Annual Report*, President and CEO Craig Lentzsch, who left Motor Coach Industries in November 1994, emphasized Greyhound's history as he reflected on the company's $77.4 million loss and "financial restructuring." Despite the significantly lower passenger totals he declared, "Our business is as crucial to the American way of life today as it was decades ago when this company helped immigrants seek a better life and delivered thousands of soldiers home to their families." While asserting, "Greyhound Lines has an historic and essential role in connecting rural America to urban America," he also offered a cautionary reminder: "Tradition, however, is not enough to carry a company."

Continuing the unsuccessful search for a meaningful identity, Greyhound's 1995 *Annual Report*, while acknowledging a $17.8 million loss, declared, "In January of 1995, we began to implement a back-to-the-basics approach to the business. In the process, we rediscovered what makes Greyhound so important to our customers: We provide a unique service by allowing them to travel where they want, when they want, at a price they can afford." Greyhound identified its "core passengers" as those with incomes of up to $15,000. They represented 44 percent of Greyhound's passenger revenue. "Transitional passengers," with incomes between $15,000 and $50,000, constituted the other 56 percent of revenue. These are passengers that "have the disposable income to switch or make the 'transition' from one mode of transportation to another." The 1995 *Annual Report* concluded that "the road ahead" required returning to "basic principles" defined as "going back to its roots as a low-cost transportation leader."

Fig. 232. 1988 Eagle Model 15. *AACA*

These continual nods to tradition by Greyhound's leadership actually failed to draw relevant lessons from the past and also failed to recognize the limitations of defining travel primarily in terms of the cost for the traveler. Roland Marchand's analysis of advertising, noted earlier, suggests roads not taken in Greyhound's efforts to develop a meaningful identity. His assertion that "People prefer to identify with portrayals of themselves as they aspire to be" suggests that as in the past, growth for Greyhound would require travel beyond necessity. During this period, Greyhound did not offer portrayals of aspiration—images of what people wished they were—but images of what people actually were. Greyhound's identity needed to reflect dreams as well as reality, two sides of the same coin.

Greyhound's 1996 *Annual Report* asserted success "comes from understanding the needs of our customers." Specifically, "Market research studies show that Greyhound passengers are different than airline passengers in that most decide to travel only a short time before their trip and purchase their tickets on the day of travel. We must manage our resources to get these people where they want to go, when they want to go and at a price they can afford." The 1996 *Annual Report* also acknowledged the 1995 effort that "redefined Greyhound as an intercity bus company serving the needs of a growing and underserved customer base." In the past Greyhound grew as it found ways to encourage travel by the increasingly affluent working and middle classes. In 1997, Greyhound publicity asserted, "We know that the biggest competitor for our core customer's travel dollar is not the airlines or even the car, it's the issue of affordability." The "redefinition" effort of the 1980s and 1990s indicates Greyhound sought growth among the less affluent "underserved." The specific identification of Greyhound's "underserved" travelers as "working people on a budget, students, senior citizens, and vacationers from a wide variety of ethnic backgrounds," reflects an attention to demographics absent in the past when Greyhound advertisements featured white middle class travelers. Laudatory from a social justice perspective, the effort to increase revenue through greater travel by the less affluent was nonetheless problematic.

Reflecting the the difficulties inherent in this strategy, Canadian-based Laidlaw Inc. acquired Greyhound, in mid-March 1999. Laidlaw's 1999 *Annual Report* offered these observations. "Greyhound's primary customer base comprises travelers with family incomes of under $35,000—about 50% of U.S. households. Greyhound's major competing transportation mode is the family car. Airline discount fare programs can also sporadically affect passenger loads." The *Report* indicated Laidlaw intended to expand tourism and package delivery services "using the power of the Greyhound platform." By 2001, however, Laidlaw declared bankruptcy, emerging from Chapter 11 reorganization by mid-2003, relocating to Naperville, Illinois, while Greyhound headquarters remained in Dallas.

As a response to continual financial difficulties, Greyhound implemented downsizing measures including cutting service in rural areas, focusing on medium-haul trips of less than 450 miles. Media accounts, while acknowledging the need for Greyhound to do something to survive, often lamented

MCI Model 102D3. *GBM*

these cutbacks in service, focusing on individuals who relied on Greyhound to get to the doctor, visit relatives, or travel to and from home to college. Seeking to put the effort into perspective, *Fortune*, September 6, 2004, noted, "Still, modern market forces, while they may be efficient, aren't kind: Greyhound's pullback leaves big holes in the frayed network of rural mass transportation."

In addition to cutting back service to unprofitable areas, Greyhound also continued to seek and promote a viable identity. *Crain's Chicago Business*, September 6, 2004, covered Greyhound's new advertising campaign to convince "young people that riding the bus is cool." The article quoted Steve Kane, publisher and editor of *Bus Ride* who asserted, "There's the perception that terminals are on the wrong side of the tracks and that it's not exactly an upscale mode of transportation." The article also noted, "Others say Greyhound's main challenge can't necessarily be helped by advertising. 'It's one thing to change an ad idea; it's another to get that reflected in the customer's experience—the condition of the buses or the terminals and so on,' says Allen Adamson, managing director at [advertising agency] Landor Associates."

Media coverage often reflected a distinct dichotomy in the way people view Greyhound as a cultural icon, acknowledging the real failures and shortcomings while at the same time wistfully harkening back to Greyhound's better days. For example, the

MCI Model 102D3. *GBM*

Prevost H3-45 operated by Greyhound Canada. *AACA*

Charleston [South Carolina] *Post and Courier*, October 12, 2005, described Greyhound as "a flabby, old company struggling to keep up in the competitive transportation industry." The article also declared, "Greyhound coaches wheezed and sighed through folk anthems, Jack Kerouac novels and the dreams of countless small-town runaways—cultivating America's wanderlust in corners of the country where railroads didn't go."

Lynda Edwards, writing in the April 27, 2005 *Arizona Daily Star* observed, "When Greyhound Lines Inc. launched its 41-passenger 'Highway Traveler,' in 1953, travel posters swooned all over the bus's picture windows and on-board bathrooms. The posters flaunted photos of fathers in suits and mothers in poufy taffeta hustling children through terminals that looked like glass and steel temples. Cheap airfares and urban decay drained most of the reality from that picture long ago."

Jim Pollock, writing in the Des Moines *Business Record*, July 12, 2004, while admitting, "I don't expect to ever ride a Greyhound again," offered this nostalgic remembrance of better days gone by. "Greyhound buses ran right past our house twice a day when I was a kid in State Center, one heading east and one heading west. I would read the destination signs above the windshields—San Francisco, Denver, New York—and marvel at this connection to the outside world." Writers often deplore the state of Greyhound facilities, but for Pollock something less was more. "In those days you caught the bus at Watson's Grocery Store, a bit of Americana even then. It featured a wonderfully creaky wood floor, beautiful wood cabinets, a spool of string over the counter for wrapping bundles and a photograph of Dwight Eisenhower that stayed on the wall as lesser presidents came and went."

A comparison of song lyrics offers another measure of Greyhound's declining status. In 1947, "Love on a Greyhound Bus," told the story of two passengers who "cuddled up close" and "fell in love on a Greyhound bus." By 2001, the romance of the road reflected different circumstances. According to *Billboard* magazine, March 1, 2001, "Backseat of a Greyhound Bus," performed by country singer Sara Evans, told "the story of an unwed mother who flees a small-minded small town and winds up giving birth—you guessed it—on the back seat of a Greyhound bus between Jackson, Miss., and Memphis."

Despite the decline in the number of those riding the bus and the decline in its status, Greyhound continues to motor on—the British firm, FirstGroup PLC, acquired Laidlaw International in February 2007—and *most importantly*, to remain a cultural icon. The durability of this perception reflects the success of Greyhound's promotional efforts. The public's acceptance of its iconic status means Greyhound continues to exist as something beyond reality, something larger than life. While the reality of a less-romantic road plays a part in the mind of the public, Greyhound also exists in the imagination. In spite of cultural changes that continue to affect Greyhound, a part of the icon refuses to conform to reality. In our imagination and dreams, "Going the Greyhound Way" is forever the means to experience "The Romance of the Road."

AUTOMOTIVE

AMC Cars 1954-1987: An Illustrated History ISBN 1-58388-112-3
AMC Performance Cars 1951-1983 Photo Archive ISBN 1-58388-127-1
AMX Photo Archive: From Concept to Reality ISBN 1-58388-062-3
The American Taxi- A Century of Service ISBN 1-58388-176-X
Avanti: The Complete Story ISBN 1-58388-213-8
Buick 1946-1960 Photo Archive ISBN 1-58388-178-6
Cadillac Fleetwood Series Seventy-Five Limousines Photo Archive ISBN 1-58388-248-0
Cadillac: The Tailfin Years ISBN 1-58388-212-X
Camaro 1967-2000 Photo Archive ISBN 1-58388-032-1
Checker Cab Co. Photo History ISBN 1-58388-100-X
Chevrolet Corvair Photo History ISBN 1-58388-118-2
Chevrolet Station Wagons 1946-1966 Photo Archive ISBN 1-58388-069-0
Classic American Limousines 1955-2000 Photo Archive ISBN 1-58388-041-0
Cobra and Shelby Mustang Photo Archive 1962-2007 Including Prototypes and Clones ISBN 1-58388-198-0
The Complete U.S. Automotive Sales Literature Checklist 1946-2000 ISBN 1-58388-155-7
Corvair by Chevrolet Experimental & Production Cars 1957-1969, Ludvigsen Library Series ISBN 1-58388-058-5
Corvette The Exotic Experimental Cars, Ludvigsen Library Series ISBN 1-58388-017-8
Corvette Prototypes & Show Cars Photo Album ISBN 1-882256-77-8
DeTomaso Pantera ISBN 1-58388-177-8
Duesenberg Racecars and Passenger Cars Photo Archive ISBN 1-58388-145-X
Encyclopedia of Small-Scale Diecast Motor Vehicle Manufacturers ISBN 1-58388-174-3
Ferrari- The Factory Maranello's Secrets 1950-1975, Ludvigsen Library Series ISBN 1-58388-085-2
Ford Postwar Flatheads 1946-1953 Photo Archive ISBN 1-58388-080-1
Ford Station Wagons 1929-1991 Photo History ISBN 1-58388-103-4
Grand Prix: Pontiac's Luxury Performance Car ISBN 1-58388-184-0
Henney Motor Company: A Complete Story ISBN 1-58388-233-2
Hudson Automobiles 1934-1957 Photo Archive ISBN 1-58388-110-7
Imperial 1964-1968 Photo Archive ISBN 1-882256-23-9
It's Delightful! It's Delovely! It's DeSoto Automobiles ISBN 1-58388-172-7
Jaguar XK120, XK140, XK150 Sports Cars Ludvigsen Library Series ISBN 1-58388-150-6
Javelin Photo Archive: From Concept to Reality ISBN 1-58388-071-2
Kaiser-Frazer 1947-1955 Photo Archive ISBN 1-58388-239-1
The Lincoln Continental Story: From Zephyr to Mark II ISBN 1-58388-154-9
Lincoln Motor Cars 1920-1942 Photo Archive ISBN 1-882256-57-3
Mercedes-Benz 300SL: Gullwings and Roadsters 1954-1964 Ludvigsen Library Series ISBN 1-58388-137-9
Mercury Automobiles 1939-1959 ISBN 1-58388-205-7
MG Saloons and Coupes 1925-1980 ISBN 1-58388-144-1
Nash 1936-1957 Photo Archive ISBN 1-58388-086-0
Oldsmobile 1946-1960 Photo Archive ISBN 1-58388-168-9
Packard Motor Cars 1946-1958 Photo Archive ISBN 1-882256-45-X
Pontiac Dream Cars, Show Cars & Prototypes 1928-1998 Photo Album ISBN 1-882256-93-X
Pontiac's Greatest Decade 1959-1969—The Wide Track Era: An Illustrated History ISBN 1-58388-163-8
Rambler 1950-1969 Photo Archive ISBN 1-58388-078-X
Stretch Limousines 1928-2001 Photo Archive ISBN 1-58388-070-4
Studebaker Lark 1959-1966 Photo Archive ISBN 1-58388-107-7
The Collector's Guide to GTO 1964-1974 ISBN 1-58388-196-4
Thirty Years of the Volkswagen Golf & Rabbit ISBN 1-58388-158-1
Ultimate Corvette Trivia Challenge ISBN 1-58388-035-6

BUSES

Buses of ACF Photo Archive Including ACF-Brill And CCF-Brill ISBN 1-58388-101-8
Buses of Motor Coach Industries 1932-2000 Photo Archive ISBN 1-58388-039-9
Buses of Western Flyer and New Flyer Industries Photo Archive ISBN 1-58388-229-4
City Transit Buses of the 20th Century Photo Gallery ISBN 1-58388-146-8
Fageol & Twin Coach Buses 1922-1956 Photo Archive ISBN 1-58388-075-5
Flxible Intercity Buses 1924-1970 Photo Archive ISBN 1-58388-108-5
Flxible Transit Buses 1953-1995 Photo Archive ISBN 1-58388-053-4
GM Intercity Coaches 1944-1980 Photo Archive ISBN 1-58388-099-2
Going the Greyhound Way: The Romance of the Road ISBN 1-58388-246-4
Greyhound in Postcards: Buses, Depots and Posthouses ISBN 1-58388-130-1
Highway Buses of the 20th Century Photo Gallery ISBN 1-58388-121-2
Mack® Buses 1900-1960 Photo Archive* ISBN 1-58388-020-8
New York City Transit Buses 1945-1975 Photo Archive ISBN 1-58388-149-2
New York Fifth Avenue Coach Co. 1885-1960 ISBN 1-58388-249-9
Prevost Buses 1924-2002 Photo Archive ISBN 1-58388-083-6
Rapid Transit Series Buses: General Motors and Beyond ISBN 1-58388-209-X
Trailways Buses 1936-2001 Photo Archive ISBN 1-58388-029-1
Trolley Buses 1913-2001 Photo Archive ISBN 1-58388-057-7
Trolley Buses Around the World: A Photo Gallery ISBN 1-58388-175-1
Welcome Aboard the GM New Look Bus: An Enthusiast's Reference ISBN 1-58388-167-5
Yellow Coach Buses 1923-1943 Photo Archive ISBN 1-58388-054-2

RAILWAYS

American Passenger Trains: WWII to Amtrak ISBN 1-58388-232-4
Chicago & North Western Passenger Trains of the 400 Fleet Photo Archive ISBN 1-58388-159-X
Chicago Stations & Trains Photo Archive ISBN 1-58388-216-2
Chicago, St. Paul, Minneapolis & Omaha Railway 1880-1940 Photo Archive ISBN 1-882256-67-0
Chicagoland Commuter Railroads: Metra & Northern Indiana Commuter Transportation District ISBN 1-58388-190-5
Classic Sreamliners Photo Archive: The Trains and the Designers ISBN 1-58388-144-x
Freight Trains of the Upper Mississippi River Photo Archive ISBN 1-58388-136-0
Great Lakes Ore Docks and Ore Cars ISBN 1-58388-202-2
Great Northern Railway Ore Docks of Lake Superior Photo Archive ISBN 1-58388-073-9
Illinois Central Railroad 1854-1960 Photo Archive ISBN 1-58388-063-1
Interurban Trains to Chicago Photo Archive ISBN 1-58388-199-9
Locomotives of the Upper Midwest Photo Archive: Diesel Power in the 1960s and 1970s ISBN 1-58388-113-1
Milwaukee Road 1850-1960 Photo Archive ISBN 1-882256-61-1
Milwaukee Road Depots 1856-1954 Photo Archive ISBN 1-58388-040-2
Northern Pacific Railway Photo Archive ISBN 1-58388-186-7
Pacific Coast Commuter Railroads: From San Diego to Anchorage ISBN 1-58388-221-9
Pennsylvania Railroad Locomotives: Steam, Diesel & Electric Photo Archive ISBN 1-58388-228-6
Rio Grande Locomotives Photo Archive ISBN 1-58388-244-8
Show Trains of the 20th Century ISBN 1-58388-030-5
Soo Line 1975-1992 Photo Archive ISBN 1-882256-68-9
Steam Locomotives of the B&O Railroad Photo Archive ISBN 1-58388-095-X
Trains of the Circus 1872-1956 ISBN 1-58388-024-0
Trains of the Upper Midwest Photo Archive Steam & Diesel in the 1950s & 1960s ISBN 1-58388-036-4
Union Pacific Railroad- Passenger Trains of the City Fleet Photo Archive ISBN 1-58388-236-7
Washington State Railroad Depots Photo Archive ISBN 1-58388-245-6

TRUCKS

4x4 Offroad Racing Trucks ISBN 1-58388-243-X
AM General: Hummers, Mutts, Buses & Postal Jeeps ISBN 1-58388-135-2
Autocar Trucks of the 1950s At Work ISBN 1-58388-231-6
Autocar Trucks of the 1960s At Work ISBN 1-58388-241-3
Autocar Trucks 1899-1950 Photo Archive ISBN 1-58388-115-8
Brockway Trucks 1948-1961 Photo Archive* ISBN 1-882256-55-7
Chevrolet El Camino Photo History Incl. GMC Sprint & Caballero ISBN 1-58388-044-5
Circus and Carnival Trucks 1923-2000 Photo Archive ISBN 1-58388-048-8
Diamond T Trucks 1911-1966 Photo Archive ISBN 1-58388-204-9
Dodge C-Series Trucks Restorer's & Collector's Reference Guide and History ISBN 1-58388-140-9
Dodge Heavy-Duty Trucks 1928-1975 ISBN 1-58388-194-8
Dodge Pickups 1939-1978 Photo Album ISBN 1-882256-82-4
Dodge Ram Trucks 1994-2001 Photo History ISBN 1-58388-051-8
Dodge Trucks 1948-1960 Photo Archive ISBN 1-882256-37-9
El Camino by Chevrolet ISBN 1-58388-215-4
Federal Trucks Photo Archive ISBN 1-58388-223-5
Ford Heavy-Duty Trucks 1948-1998 Photo History ISBN 1-58388-043-7
Ford Medium-Duty Trucks 1917-1998 Photo History ISBN 1-58388-162-X
Ford Ranchero 1957-1979 Photo History ISBN 1-58388-126-3
Freightliner Trucks 1937-1981 Photo Archive ISBN 1-58388-090-9
FWD Trucks 1910-1974 Photo Archive ISBN 1-58388-142-5
GMC Heavy-Duty Trucks 1927-1987 ISBN 1-58388-125-5
GMC Light-Duty Trucks ISBN 1-58388-191-3
International Heavy Trucks of the 1950s: At Work ISBN 1-58388-160-3
International Heavy Trucks of the 1960s: At Work ISBN 1-58388-161-1
Jeep 1941-2000 Photo Archive ISBN 1-58388-021-6
Jeep Prototypes & Concept Vehicles Photo Archive ISBN 1-58388-033-X
Kenworth Trucks 1950-1979 At Work ISBN 1-58388-147-6
Land Rover: The Incomparable 4x4 from Series 1 to Defender, Ludvigsen Library Series ISBN 1-58388-179-4
Mack Model AB Photo Archive* ISBN 1-882256-18-2
Mack AP Super-Duty Trucks 1926-1938 Photo Archive* ISBN 1-882256-54-9
Mack Model B 1953-1966 Volume 2 Photo Archive* ISBN 1-882256-34-4
Mack EB-EC-ED-EE-EF-EG-DE 1936-1951 Photo Archive* ISBN 1-882256-29-8
Mack FC-FCSW-NW 1936-1947 Photo Archive* ISBN 1-882256-28-X
Mack LF-LH-LJ-LM-LT 1940-1956 Photo Archive* ISBN 1-882256-38-7
Muscle Trucks: High-Performance Pickups ISBN 1-58388-197-2
Peterbilt Trucks 1939-1979 At Work ISBN 1-58388-152-2
Refuse Trucks Photo Archive ISBN 1-58388-042-9
Reo Trucks 1910-1966 Photo Archive ISBN 1-58388-181-6
Semi Trucks of the 1950s: A Photo Gallery ISBN 1-58388-187-5
Studebaker Trucks 1927-1940 Photo Archive ISBN 1-882256-40-9
The Long Haul: American Trucking Companies ISBN 1-58388-211-1
White Trucks of the 1950s At Work ISBN 1-58388-230-8
White Trucks of the 1960s At Work ISBN 1-58388-240-5
White Trucks 1900-1937 Photo Archive ISBN 1-882256-80-8

More Great Titles From

Iconografix

All Iconografix books are available from direct mail specialty book dealers and bookstores worldwide, or can be ordered from the publisher. For book trade and distribution information or to add your name to our mailing list and receive a **FREE CATALOG** contact:

Iconografix, Inc.
PO Box 446, Dept BK, Hudson, WI, 54016

Telephone: (715) 381-9755,
(800) 289-3504 (USA), Fax: (715) 381-9756
info@iconografixinc.com
www.iconografixinc.com